THE WRATH OF
A LOVING GOD

BY THE SAME AUTHOR:

The Pilgrim God: A Biblical Journey
(Washington: Pastoral, 1985 / Dublin: Veritas, 1990)

The Way of the Lord: A New Testament Pilgrimage
(Washington: Pastoral, 1990 / Dublin: Veritas, 1990)

Praying the Our Father Today
(Washington: Pastoral, 1992)

God of the Unexpected: Newness and the Spirit in the Bible
(London: Mowbray, 1995)

The Adventure of Holiness:
Biblical Foundations and Present-Day Perspectives
(New York: Alba House, 1999)

At the Wellspring: Jesus and the Samaritan Woman
(New York: Alba House, 2001)

Reading the Ten Commandments Anew:
Towards a Land of Freedom
(New York: Alba House, 2004)

I Am the Beginning and the End:
Creation Stories and Visions of Fulfilment in the Bible
(New York: Alba House, 2007)

Friends in Christ:
Reimagining the Christian Church in an Age of Globalization
(Maryknoll: Orbis, 2012)

Life on the Edge:
Holy Saturday and the Recovery of the End Time
(Eugene, OR: Wipf & Stock, 2017)

182862

THE WRATH OF A LOVING GOD

Unraveling a Biblical Conundrum

Brother John of Taizé

Gellart Memorial Library

Menlo Park, CA 94025

DISCARD

library.stpsu.edu

CASCADE *Books* · Eugene, Oregon

THE WRATH OF A LOVING GOD
Unraveling a Biblical Conundrum

Copyright © 2019 SARL Ateliers et Presses de Taizé, Communauté de
Taizé CS 10004, 71250 Taizé, France. All rights reserved. Except for brief
quotations in critical publications or reviews, no part of this book may
be reproduced in any manner without prior written permission from the
publisher. Write: Permissions, Wipf and Stock Publishers, 199 W. 8th Ave.,
Suite 3, Eugene, OR 97401.

Cascade Books
An Imprint of Wipf and Stock Publishers
199 W. 8th Ave., Suite 3
Eugene, OR 97401

www.wipfandstock.com

PAPERBACK ISBN: 978-1-5326-7072-5
HARDCOVER ISBN: 978-1-5326-7073-2
EBOOK ISBN: 978-1-5326-7074-9

Cataloguing-in-Publication data:

Names: Brother John of Taizé, author.
Title: The wrath of a loving god : unraveling a biblical conundrum /
    Brother John of Taizé.
Description: Eugene, OR: Cascade Books, 2019 | Includes bibliographical
    references and index.
Identifiers: ISBN 978-1-5326-7072-5 (paperback) | ISBN 978-1-5326-7073-2
    (hardcover) | ISBN 978-1-5326-7074-9 (ebook)
Subjects: LCSH: God (Christianity)—Wrath—Biblical teaching. | Grace
    (Theology)—Biblical teaching. | God (Christianity)—Love—Biblical
    teaching.
Classification: BT153.W7 B76 2019 (print) | BT153.W7 (ebook)

Manufactured in the U.S.A.   OCTOBER 2, 2019

Published in French by Ateliers et Presses de Taizé, 2018 under the title *La colère d'un Dieu d'amour: Déchiffrer une énigme biblique.*

Contents

List of Biblical Books Quoted xi

PRELUDE: *An Angry God?* 1
The Wrong Track 2
Learning How to Read the Bible 4
A Story of Liberation 7
A Theology of Anger? 9

CHAPTER I: *The Genealogy of Divine Anger* 11
The Journey of the Ark 12
And Now, Anger 14
The Rider of the Clouds 16
An Ambiguous Energy 19

CHAPTER II: *Understanding Human Anger* 22
The Wrath of the King 23
The Risks of Repression 26
Expressing the No 28
A Capital Sin? 30
A Dangerous or Constructive Reaction? 32

CHAPTER III: *Prophetic Anger* 36
Amos 37
Isaiah 39

Hosea and Jeremiah 43
Anger Interiorized 47

CHAPTER IV: *Explanatory Anger and its Critics* 51
The Deuteronomic History 52
Innocent, but Condemned 55
A God Slow to Anger 59

Intermezzo 66

CHAPTER V: *A Destabilizing Force* 71
Saved from the Wrath 72
The Day of Judgment 76
The Storm Is Coming 80
A Harsh and Dreadful Love 83
Changing Our Outlook 86

CHAPTER VI: *The Man of Sorrows* 89
Preliminary Difficulties 90
Jesus' No 90
A Provocative Act 93
From Anger to Sorrow 94
The Other Side of Anger 97
My Soul Is Sorrowful to the Point of Death 99
Happy Those Who Mourn 102

CODA: *The Wrath of the Lamb* 107
How to Read the Apocalypse 107
The Self-Destruction of Evil 109
A Paradoxical Victory 113
The Great Day of Wrath 114

Bibliography 121
Other Works Consulted 123
Scripture Index 125

List of Biblical Books Quoted

Gen	Genesis
Exod	Exodus
Num	Numbers
Deut	Deuteronomy
Josh	Joshua
Judg	Judges
1 Sam	1 Samuel
2 Sam	2 Samuel
1 Kgs	1 Kings
2 Kgs	2 Kings
1 Chr	1 Chronicles
2 Chr	2 Chronicles
Neh	Nehemiah
Job	Job
Ps	Psalms
Prov	Proverbs
Isa	Isaiah
Jer	Jeremiah
Lam	Lamentations
Ezek	Ezekiel
Dan	Daniel
Hos	Hosea
Amos	Amos
Jonah	Jonah
Zeph	Zephaniah
Zech	Zechariah
Mal	Malachi

Song	Song of Songs
Qoh	Qoheleth/Ecclesiastes
Sir	Sirach/Ecclesiasticus
Matt	Matthew
Mark	Mark
Luke	Luke
John	John
Rom	Romans
1 Cor	1 Corinthians
2 Cor	2 Corinthians
Gal	Galatians
Eph	Ephesians
Phil	Philippians
Col	Colossians
1 Thess	1 Thessalonians
2 Thess	2 Thessalonians
2 Tim	2 Timothy
Heb	Hebrews
Jas	James
1 Pet	1 Peter
2 Pet	2 Peter
1 John	1 John
Rev	Revelation

Mark 14:36 par = Mark ch. 14, v. 36 and the parallel texts in Matthew and Luke

All biblical translations, unless otherwise noted, are by the author.

Prelude

An Angry God?

IS IT NOT EVIDENT that, in our day, one of the main obstacles to understanding the biblical message is the portrait of a wrathful and vengeful God that some people claim to find in the pages of the Bible, notably in the Hebrew Scriptures, the Old Testament of Christians? It must be admitted that the collective unconscious of the inhabitants of Western countries that are traditionally Christian is populated with such images. And it goes without saying that such a vision of God is distasteful to many people of good will, interested in spirituality, who are looking for meaning in their lives, and so represents a formidable obstacle to accepting a biblical faith. But believers themselves usually do not know how to deal with those texts where God is presented as full of rage and jealous of his honor. Here are two typical passages, chosen more or less at random:

> Nevertheless, the Lord did not turn away from the heat of his fierce anger, which burned against Judah because of all that Manasseh had done to arouse his anger. So the Lord said, "I will remove Judah also from my presence as I removed Israel, and I will reject Jerusalem, the city I chose, and this temple, about which I said, 'My Name shall be there.'" (2 Kgs 23:26–27 NIV)

> Therefore the Lord's anger burns against his people;
> his hand is raised and he strikes them down.

1

The mountains shake,
and the dead bodies are like refuse in the streets.
Yet for all this, his anger is not turned away,
his hand is still upraised. (Isa 5:25)

What relation is there between these perspectives and the God of love revealed by the carpenter of Nazareth? How can they be integrated into our understanding of the divine and its actions?

The Wrong Track

One possible solution, by far the easiest and therefore implicitly adopted by many, is simply to eliminate these difficult passages from our portrait of God. The popular version of this procedure, in large part unreflective, leads to a doubling of the divine identity. On the one hand we have the deity of the Old Testament, an exacting and irritable God, and on the other the God of Jesus Christ, overflowing with kindness and tenderness. Even a mind as brilliant and enlightened as that of the philosopher Simone Weil (1909–43) did not escape this kind of facile simplification. She wrote that she could not understand "how it was possible for a rational mind to see the Jehovah of the Bible and the Father mentioned in the Gospel as one and the same being."[1]

Most of those who adopt this apparent solution probably do not imagine that it has a long history. It does not date from yesterday. At the beginning of the second century of the Common Era, a man was born in Asia Minor. He left his birthplace and came to Rome, where his preaching won for him a certain renown. His name was Marcion. Seeing no affinity at all between the Creator God found in the pages of the Hebrew Scriptures and the gospel of Jesus Christ, Marcion drew the logical—indeed too logical— conclusions from this incompatibility. In his eyes there were two completely independent deities: on the one hand the God of this world, an evil God, a merciless Judge who gave the Law to Israel; and on the other a good God, previously unknown, the Father of

---

1 Weil, *Pensées sans ordre*, 64, quoted in Chenavier, *Simone Weil*, 82.

Jesus. Jesus came to save us from the wicked God, which meant that he had to take us out of this evil world.

It goes without saying that, if the universe in which we live is the work of a wicked Creator, it follows that it too is evil. Marcion thus offers a simple explanation of the eternal problem of evil by affirming that it is the direct responsibility of a wicked Creator. The Savior thus comes on behalf of the good God to put an end to the dominance of this evil world, by destroying the works of its Ruler and by saving the souls of his disciples.

Although this way of thinking provides us with an explanation of evil, the price to pay for it seems far too high. We are forced totally to reject everything that exists, to turn our backs on the world as a whole and not just on its troubles and sorrows. In addition, Marcion had to deal with another difficulty: he did not find a confirmation of his views in the texts of the New Testament taken in their entirety. The Gospels are too permeated by the traditional faith in the God of Israel, "a compassionate and generous God" (Exod 34:6). This is even the case for Saint Paul. If some of Paul's affirmations, such as his critique of the Law, could seem to corroborate Marcion's approach, he is not completely trustworthy either. Using an argument which will later be employed by a host of others to justify their systems, Marcion claimed that the version of the New Testament promulgated by the Christian church was corrupt, perhaps due to the "false brothers" stigmatized by Saint Paul (cf. Gal 2:4). He thus set to work to establish a list of authentic passages, which was limited to a few of Paul's letters and part of Luke's Gospel. In the end, Marcion's theology led to the constitution of a new sect, to communities of his disciples which did not survive very long after the death of their founder. Most of the other believers, including illustrious writers and teachers such as Justin Martyr, Irenaeus, and Tertullian, reacted strongly against what they considered a mutilation of authentic faith in Jesus the Christ.

As has often been the case in the history of the church, this whole controversy had a positive result. It forced Christian thinkers to reflect more deeply on the composition of the Christian Bible and the relationship between the two Testaments. They concluded that the heritage of ancient Israel retains its value for the church of Christ; we cannot simply eliminate the passages that disturb us. The Creator and Legislator of Israel *is* the beloved Abba of Jesus Christ, as Jesus himself recognized.

The condemnation of Marcion's teachings closed off a dead-end for the Christian faith. It excludes once and for all the facile solution which consists in rejecting out of hand all the Bible texts that cause difficulty for us, notably the separation between the two Testaments. Once we have accepted this, however, our problem has still not been solved. How can we integrate into our vision of God apparently unacceptable elements like violence or anger? Can we attain an image of God that is less simplistic but which nonetheless retains the features of the "God of love" so well-testified to by Jesus in his words and his actions?

Learning How to Read the Bible

Before tackling our topic directly, it is necessary to deal first with some questions of method. In the first place, the prohibition against eliminating all the "difficult" bits from the Bible does not mean that everything must be placed on the same level. Recognizing that the Scriptures are inspired by God does not rule out the role of human beings in their composition. The biblical books did not fall ready-made from heaven like meteors. Divine inspiration takes into account the life and the intelligence of human beings, marked by their particular backgrounds and their vision of the world, which is inevitably limited. The faith of the writers and editors, like that of the women and men who people the pages of the Bible, remains imperfect. Christians confess that in Jesus alone do we find a perfect harmony between what God was doing in someone's existence and the awareness that person had of it. And even Jesus, as a true human being, experienced a growth in understanding (cf. Luke 2:40) and moments of uncertainty (cf. Matt 26:39). It is therefore all the more understandable that the words and events presented in the Scriptures communicate to us God's identity and desires for his creatures, but most often seen through a veil (cf.

2 Cor 3:12–18) or in a rudimentary mirror (cf. 1 Cor 13:12). A process of discernment is always necessary.

Similarly, the great tradition of the Christian church, both in the East and the West, has always emphasized the need for a *global* reading of the Scriptures. Inspiration is not primarily a matter of a particular passage isolated from its context; it is the biblical message taken as a whole that transmits an authentic understanding of divine realities. Two images can help to explain this.

The first is that of a mosaic that depicts a portrait. If the tesserae or tiles are not placed in the correct order, instead of a recognizable portrait all we see is a huge mess or, still worse, a caricature. The work of the artist consists in choosing and arranging the pieces correctly in order to achieve the desired result. In the same way, the different parts of Scripture must be situated correctly; they must be set in the right places in order for us to grasp the global message. This is a long-term endeavor, and one which is never complete. Some tiles, it must be admitted, are particularly hard to place. But for those who persevere, not counting on their own intelligence alone but also on the experience of believers passed down from one generation to the next, and above all on the presence of God's Spirit which brings life to what would otherwise be a dead letter (see 2 Cor 3:6), gradually the features of a face come to light. And for the disciples of Jesus the Christ, this face is obviously that of their Master, in whom "all the fullness of the divinity dwells in bodily form" (Col 2:9), since "when one turns towards the Lord, the veil is taken away" (2 Cor 3:16).

If the image of a mosaic illustrates well the global dimension of revelation, it does not integrate the dimension of *time*. The world we live in has a historical character; the present moment is not a static reality but a point moving between past and future, carrying with it a lot of baggage. God's self-communication conforms to this dynamic structure of our world. God speaks to each people and to each era in a language they can understand. In other words, God begins with realities on their level to lead them towards a deeper understanding. The fact, for example, that in ancient times God often revealed himself in the sordid realities of battle in no way implies an approval of armed struggle in itself, nor a justification of a particular military campaign. If people in ancient times saw God's hand in the unexpected victory achieved by a handful of men over a powerful oppressor, this was a way for them to begin to realize that the God of the Bible has a particular concern for the deprived, and that even overwhelming human might is unable, in the final analysis, to frustrate God's designs.

Viewed from the human side, this same truth can be expressed by saying that human beings comprehend God based on their own level of development. A useful analogy could be this: depending on their age, children understand differently what their parents say and do. Although they may not doubt that their parents love them, the comprehension they have of this evolves over time, and therefore later on they interpret differently the decisions made by their mother and father. For example, what seemed at the time to be a painful and unjustified deprivation may be viewed with hindsight as a blessing in disguise. The quip of the American humorist Mark Twain is well-known: "When I was a boy of 14, my father was so ignorant I could hardly stand to have the old man around. But when I got to be 21, I was astonished at how much the old man had learned in seven years."

It would thus not be wrong to understand Bible history, seen from a certain angle, as a vast pedagogy employed by God in order to transform his human partners into beings able to grasp more fully the divine identity and intentions. When Saint Paul writes that "when the fullness of time came, God sent his Son..." (Gal 4:4), is he not implying that, had Jesus been born earlier, people would not have had the necessary dispositions to welcome him? They would not yet have been ready. It is true that, in any case, most of his contemporaries were unable to welcome him appropriately (cf. John 1:11), nonetheless a threshold had been crossed so that some men and women were able to receive and continue his work. In short, in order to understand the Hebrew Scriptures correctly, we have to see them as an ongoing history, as a gradual development. If we try to stop the process and remain stuck at one stage, we run the risk of missing what is essential.

A Story of Liberation

God's revelation thus has an essentially historical character. This means that the inspired books do not transmit this revelation first of all through timeless truths; they are not philosophical or theological treatises. Although the Bible contains many different literary genres—poetry, legends, genealogies, etc.—it is above all a *narrative*. All the other elements take their place within a vast epic which tells the story of a particular god—who in the final analysis is revealed to be the Creator of the universe and the Master of human history—and a particular people—which is widened in the end to include the whole of humankind.

To speak of a narrative does not mean that the events and characters described are mere inventions. On the contrary, such an eventuality would contradict the claim of the story to describe the world in which we live. In this respect, and even if it does contain certain mythical elements, the world of the Bible is very different from the mythologies of many other civilizations. The Bible does not speak of things that have occurred in another place and time; it is situated squarely in the world we know, with all its limits and its contradictions.

At the same time, a narrative is not simply a chronicle of raw facts. The facts are chosen and sometimes embellished in order to create a story which, possessing its own logic, intends to communicate a message. This mix of factual and fictive, incidentally, is not simply due to the age of the text. In contemporary European society, it is apparently impossible to write history books for schools which can be used interchangeably in all the different countries. This is because every nation has its own way of looking at the same events: the choice of details, the interpretation of the motives of the actors, the evaluation of their behavior, all this varies according to the perspective of the editors; it is determined by the identity of the group in question. Thus the affirmation that we may know very little about the life of a Moses, a Muhammad, or a Charlemagne from the viewpoint of a positivist historiography, concerned only with "facts" that can be scientifically attested to, counts for very little when it comes to the role of these figures in the history of the human group of which they are the protagonists. At most, such information could refine the portrait we have of them and eliminate gross misunderstandings. But it would not change anything essential, for the human group that refers to them has already acquired its physiognomy. The identity of their founder does not depend upon a scientific reconstruction of the past but comes from their patrimony, passed down across the centuries by oral and written traditions.

Let us now attempt to sketch the main lines of the story which forms the framework for understanding the particular elements we find in the pages of the Bible. It is first and foremost a story of *liberation*. A God not linked to a particular place enters the life of men and women who are mistreated and oppressed, promising them a new life. This God transforms a ragtag collection of former slaves into a people. God bequeaths them a land where they can and must live as his people by following his ways (cf. Deut 8:6; 10:12; etc.)—in other words, by practicing justice and solidarity among themselves. More often than not, however, this "stiff-necked" people forgets their Maker and does not live according to his desires, which results in their losing their identity and inevitably leads to misfortune. Still, despite the unfaithfulness of his people, God for his part remains faithful. God keeps on sending messengers, the prophets, to remind them of his promises and to tell them how they should behave in order to benefit from these promises once again. And so, even in the darkest moments of Israel's history, a hope always remains, based not on human activity but on the identity and the presence of a trustworthy God.

For Christians, the good news announced by the disciples of Jesus the Messiah prolongs and completes this story. In the person of Jesus of Nazareth, and above all by his death and resurrection, the divine promises have been fulfilled (cf. 2 Cor 1:20), albeit in an unexpected fashion. At the same time, these promises have been widened to encompass all humanity, invited to enter into a new relationship with God through faith in God's Son. This communion with God is made concrete on earth by becoming part of a new community, the church, where human beings are called to live as brothers and sisters, children of the same Father, thereby continuing Christ's presence in the world.

This framework remains the unchanging starting-point for understanding the Bible. If a particular affirmation or story seems to contradict it, the contradiction can only be apparent. Brother Roger, the founder of Taizé, liked to compare the Bible to a letter that we have received from a close friend, written in a language in which we are not fluent. If a particular expression causes problems for us, we should realize that the difficulty comes above all from our lack of understanding, either of the language or of the author's intentions. To begin by calling into question our friend's affection for us is not a reasonable attitude. In the same way, before doubting God's love for his creation, the cornerstone of biblical revelation, we should ask ourselves whether we have understood correctly the events or the statements that at first glance seem disconcerting, and whether we have situated them correctly in the biblical epic as a whole.

A Theology of Anger?

In these pages, we are going to apply this method to the notion of divine anger or wrath. Rather than ignoring the difficult passages where this topic is mentioned, or even attempting to blunt their impact by explaining them away, we shall dare to ask a more crucial question: can this notion help us to understand the Bible's message in a deeper way? Does it reveal aspects of God and of our human condition that otherwise would remain hidden? In particular, given that we have no right to call God's love into question, what dimensions of love, if any, does God's wrath reveal? Developing such a "theology of anger" is assuredly not an easy task. But is it not a good way to ensure that we are not taking the easy way out simply by projecting onto God our own notions of love, notions that would turn out to be insufficient and thus ultimately disappointing? Trying to discover the meaning of the parts of Scripture that resist our understanding is an excellent way to deepen our faith, among other things because it obliges us to take into consideration aspects of the faith that are least in harmony with the mentality of people today. This assumes, however, that we never lose sight of the essentials of the faith, the "framework" mentioned above.

As for every biblical investigation, it is also of the utmost importance to try and understand from within the mentality of people in the ancient world, with both its strong and its weak points. What role did anger play in their existence? Did they understand it in the same way as we do? Why did they have the idea of projecting this notion onto God? Such questions alone can already help us to understand the Bible's message better, by calling our own outlook into question. We shall also attempt to see if there is a progression in the Bible in the way God's anger is spoken of: are there different theologies of anger? After having looked at the books of the Hebrew Scriptures, our Old Testament, we will follow this topic in the pages of the New Testament, to discover what transformations it undergoes in the life and message of Jesus.

CHAPTER I

The Genealogy of Divine Anger

AN ANGRY GOD? BUT what in fact is anger? One dictionary gives the following definition: "A strong emotion of the soul expressed by a violent physical and psychological reaction." We see from the outset that anger has two dimensions, an inner ("a strong emotion of the soul") and an outer one ("a violent physical and psychological reaction"). I see someone before me who has been antagonized. His face turns red; his breathing becomes heavy; he starts banging on the table. From these outward signs I conclude that he is angry, for in a similar situation I would have felt the same emotion and would have acted similarly.

In the case of a god, however, things are not so simple. Most of us have never seen a supernatural being and, in addition, we have not the faintest idea how such a being thinks, feels, or reacts. To speak of an angry God, therefore, is to take a leap into the unknown. It means that we are projecting an attitude and behavior typical of *homo sapiens* onto a being who, whether real or imaginary, is essentially different from us. Scholars call this process by which we apply human characteristics to a non-human entity *anthropomorphism*. Consequently, we must always keep in mind that the notion of divine anger is not a simple, direct observation. It is a second-level reality, the transfer of something human to another domain. In other words, it is not a fact but an *interpretation*. It is already a theology in miniature, an attempt to understand and to explain the world of the divine.

To understand the process which leads to this kind of anthropomorphism, it is best to begin with the outer dimension. What empirical events in the natural world enable us to draw the conclusion that God is enraged? Let us begin with a biblical narrative very distant from the way we see the world today, one which seems to contain quite archaic elements. Precisely because it disconcerts us, it can help us to comprehend the antecedents of divine anger.

The Journey of the Ark

This first example comes from the books of Samuel. At the center of the story there is an object, "the ark of the covenant of the Lord." The ark is a casket or box made of acacia wood (Exod 25:10–16), containing the two tablets of stone on which were written the Ten Words, the core of the Law given on Mount Sinai (Deut 10:1–5). For the ancient Israelites, it represented the presence of the Lord who accompanied them in all their wanderings (Num 10:33–36). Looked at in another way, the ark represents the throne of the invisible God, "who is seated on the cherubim" (1 Sam 4:4).

In chapters 4–6 of the first book of Samuel, the ark plays a central role. It is endowed with a dire and uncontrollable power. Underneath the surface of the story we can discern an early stage of human religiosity. In many so-called primitive cultures, certain objects—a stone, a tree, a mountain—are considered sacred. Concretely, this means that they are surrounded by great awe and reverence, because they are believed to contain a force or energy, sometimes referred to as *mana*, which is not of this world. Approaching them can thus have unexpected and even harmful consequences.

In the final version of the story that concerns us here, the one we find in our Bibles, the object in question—the ark of the Lord—is not viewed as divine in itself; its meaning comes from its link with a personal God, who has created a people and who has established a covenant with them. Still, the archaic dimension remains present, barely hidden beneath the surface. In the entire course of the narrative, God never speaks or decides anything in person. The simple mute presence of the ark is the motive force of the story. Brought into the camp of the Israelites who have just been vanquished in battle, it evokes great enthusiasm in them and throws their enemies, the Philistines, into disarray (1 Sam 4:1–11). But things do not take their expected course; Israel is defeated once again and the ark is captured by the Philistines. Its power is evidently unpredictable, not in the least at the beck and call of those who possess it.

Once in the enemy camp, the ark continues to create confusion. It destroys the statue of the god Dagon in his temple (5:1–5), and then causes a plague in the Philistine cities to which it is sent (5:6–12). Finally, the Philistines decide that they have had enough of this and must send the ark back to Israel. When it arrives at Beth-shemesh, on the border of Philistine territory, and is at first welcomed joyfully by the inhabitants, the ark keeps doing damage: "It struck down seventy (or in one version 50,070) men, and the people mourned because the Lord had inflicted such a great catastrophe on the people. The people of Beth-shemesh said, 'Who is able to stand before the Lord, the holy God?'" (6:19–20). And so they send the dreadful ark on to another city, Kiriath-jearim.

Despite some probable later reworking, this story is obviously based upon the notion of a sacred object charged with supernatural energy, which possesses a certain intentionality but which does not always follow ordinary human logic. Its simple presence in the midst of human beings turns everything upside down and causes the normal framework of society to fall apart. This is the reason why, incidentally, in most civilizations the sacred is surrounded by rules that bar access to it, in order to protect people from its redoubtable power.

Here, in the final version of the text, we see that the narrator attempts to lend a measure of rationality to the enigmatic behavior of the ark by attributing a motive to the death of the men: "He struck down the men of Beth-shemesh, *because they looked upon the ark of the Lord*" (6:19a). Implicitly, the author introduces the categories of offense and punishment into the story, and in so doing he turns it into a moral tale, however rudimentary and indeed incomprehensible it may in fact be, since it is not immediately obvious why the simple fact of looking at an object would be punishable by death. In any event, by this procedure the narrator intends to indicate a *meaning*, so that the activity of God's ark is not simply seen as arbitrary, as we might imagine at first sight.

And Now, Anger

In the second book of Samuel, the journey of the ark continues once again during the reign of the great king David. Having defeated the Philistines and all the enemies of Israel in the land, the king selects Jerusalem as his capital city and, to indicate clearly the link with the traditional faith, he decides to bring the ark into the city and to establish it there. The editor of what is customarily known as the Deuteronomic history, which comprises the biblical books from Joshua to Kings, is careful once again to relate the ark to Israel's God. It is "the ark of God, called by the name of the God of hosts, seated upon the cherubim" (2 Sam 6:2). Still, this ark retains its unpredictable and disconcerting character. During the procession to transport it to its new dwelling place, we read:

> They came to the threshing-floor of Nakon. Uzza stretched out his hand to the ark of God and took hold of it, because the oxen were about to let it fall. God's anger was kindled against Uzza, and God struck him down there because of his disrespect. He died right there next to the ark of God. (2 Sam 6:6–7)

This divine outburst of temper then awakens, by a kind of ricochet effect, an outburst of anger in David (6:8), as well as fear. He decides to abandon his attempt to transport the ark and leaves it in the home of a foreigner, Oved-Edom. But once settled there, the ark changes its behavior. Through it Oved-Edom's household is blessed (6:11–12) so that David, relieved, can finally bring the ark to Jerusalem amidst music, dancing, and the joyful shouts of the crowd. The ark no longer awakens in him negative emotions, but rather a joy that he cannot keep for himself and that shows itself by a spontaneous dance.

Now if we read verses 6 and 7 by themselves, detached from the rest of the story of the ark recounted in these books, we find ourselves in the presence of a classic example of the "evil God" noted by Marcion and many others. God loses his temper at a poor individual whose only fault was to put his hand on the ark in order to keep it from falling to the ground, which would, incidentally, have been a sacrilege of the first order. God does not only seem to us irrational, but unjust to boot. The punishment—death—seems far out of proportion to the crime, if indeed there was any crime at all.

If we return to the probable origins of the text, however, its apparent irrationality becomes comprehensible. Anger is mentioned only once in the story, in verse 7; it is thus in all probability an addition by the editor of the final version of the narrative, especially since, as we shall see later, divine anger is a popular explanatory device of the Deuteronomic school. This verse would then be, as in 1 Samuel 6:19a, a later interpretation to explain and justify this surprising death. It attempts to lend a measure of rationality, a meaning, to an event which in itself is not rational.

In fact, the rabbinical and Christian commentaries on the story go even further in their attempt to explain the objective offense of Uzza, the fact that he profaned a holy object. In this way they strive to justify God's behavior, to acquit the deity of any accusation of being arbitrary and unjust. Ironically, their efforts have precisely the opposite effect for us today. The implicit background of the story, that of an object charged with impersonal energy, would in the final analysis create fewer difficulties for the modern mentality. Uzza would then be comparable to someone who touches a high-voltage electrical line and is immediately electrocuted. No question of intentionality would be involved, but rather a simple physical relationship of cause and effect. Obviously, in that case the personal dimension of the divine would recede into the background. And, to anticipate one of the main arguments of this book, here we encounter the key dilemma of any theology of God's anger: it employs a characteristic drawn from the life of human beings to explain a reality which is to a great extent infra-personal. A too "personal" anger runs the risk of disfiguring the God of the Bible, whereas an anger which is too "impersonal" leaves God out of the picture. The biblical theologies of anger vacillate between these two extremes, while awaiting their reconciliation in the mystery of Christ.

The Rider of the Clouds

Let us return to our main argument. The story of the ark shows us one experience underlying the notion of anger applied to God. It has to do with an uncommon power or force that "explodes" and causes damage when confronted with certain human situations. In addition, this force is not considered as belonging to our world here below; it has its source elsewhere, in the world of the sacred.

In the story of the ark's journey, the causes of these explosions of energy are not made explicit; they are apparently not linked to any particular cosmic or human events. The ark appears, and everything else seems to follow from this. Elsewhere in the Bible, however, God's coming is linked to natural phenomena. A list of these phenomena is found in the first book of Kings, at the very moment when they are seen to be insufficient. The prophet Elijah, deeply discouraged, goes on pilgrimage to Horeb, the mountain of God:

> The Lord said, "Go out and stand on the mountain before the Lord; the Lord is passing by." A great and mighty wind, tearing apart the mountains and shattering the cliffs, was before the Lord; but the Lord was not in the wind. After the wind, an earthquake; but the Lord was not in the earthquake. And after the earthquake, a fire; but the Lord was not in the fire. (1 Kings 19:11–12)

The classical signs of the divine presence pass before Elijah: wind, earthquake, and fire. The fact that in this particular case the

Lord was not present in these signs would have astonished the hearers of the story, because they would have expected a manifestation of the divine to take place in precisely this way. All these phenomena come together perfectly in the experience of a *storm*. It should not astonish us that, in many ancient civilizations, this kind of natural event—powerful winds, thunder, lightning, rain and hail—was viewed as an epiphany of the divine. Among the deities in the land of Canaan, invaded then conquered by the Israelites, was the god Baal, worshipped as a storm-god. One of Baal's titles, Rider of the Clouds, was given to the God of Israel in Psalm 68, a song which incidentally contains many archaic elements. For example, the Lord leaves his dwelling place, his holy mountain, like a king who goes out to conquer the world in the midst of cosmic upheavals:

> God, when you went out at the head of your people,
> when you marched in the wilderness,
> the earth quaked, and the heavens poured water,
> before God, the God of Sinai,
> before God, the God of Israel.
> God, you caused plentiful rain to fall.
> (Ps 68:7–9)

And later in this same song, a victory procession that evokes the journey of the ark is mentioned:

> They saw your processions, God,
> the processions of my God, my king, into the holy place,
> the singers in front, the musicians behind,
> in the middle the maidens beating their drums.
> (Ps 68:24–25)

Psalm 29, which also contains Canaanean motifs, describes God by means of images of thunder ("The powerful voice of the Lord, the majestic voice of the Lord, the Lord's voice breaks the cedars," vv. 4–5) and lightning ("The Lord's voice strikes with blades of fire," v. 7) that cause the earth to quake (vv. 8–9).

It is understandable that, in that long-ago age, powerful upheavals of nature, violent and often unpredictable, seemed to witness to an unbridled energy that could only come from the world of the gods. And yet it should be added that such manifestations were not necessarily negative. All these natural phenomena are in themselves ambiguous. If a tempest can frighten and cause damage, a sudden rainstorm after months of drought brings obvious relief and allows life to go on. Psalm 29, just mentioned above, concludes not with a disaster or a war but with these words:

> The Lord will give strength to his people,
> the Lord will bless his people with *shalom* [peace, prosperity].
> (Ps 29:11)

Similarly, wind can be both destructive and beneficial. And even fire, the most universal symbol of holiness, has this twofold character. Though it can be dangerous—so one should not get too close—it brings light and heat, makes cooking possible, and keeps away wild beasts during the night. We should not forget that, when God showed himself to Moses at the beginning of the Exodus from Egypt, he did so "in a flame of fire, from the middle of a bush . . . The bush was on fire but the bush was not consumed" (Exod 3:2), as if to emphasize that God's power is certainly uncontrollable, but basically beneficial.

The "explosive" and destructive side of God's coming is manifested above all when it involves a confrontation with the enemies of Israel. In Psalm 83, for example, the author exhorts God to use his power against the nation's traditional enemies, who want to wipe them out:

> O God, make them like dust whirling in the wind
> like a fire that burns the forest,
> like a flame setting the hills ablaze.
> Thus you will pursue them with your tempest,
> and with your storm dismay them.
> (Ps 83:13–15)

God's victory over the Egyptian army during the exodus from Egypt is described using similar images:

> By the breath of your nostrils
> the waters were heaped up,

the flowing waters stood up like a wall,
the deeps were hardened in the heart of the sea. . . .
You blew your wind, and the sea covered them,
they sank like lead in the mighty waters.
(Exod 15:8–10)

Here a further step is taken. As we shall see, the most common way anger is expressed in Hebrew is by using the word "nostrils" or "nose." So an alternative translation of the phrase "by the breath of your nostrils" could be "by the force of your anger." The act by which God defends his people by a mighty wind thus calls to mind an outburst of fury against their enemies. We are already on the road to anthropomorphism.

An Ambiguous Energy

Compared to our modern languages, ancient Hebrew is still very rooted in the sensible world. Most of the roots of the words have several meanings, the first of which are infallibly concrete. To express anger, the most common verb is *ḥrh*, which means first of all "to burn, be kindled." Then there is the verb *'nph*, "to breathe heavily," which is related to the noun *'aph*, "nostril, nose." This last word is the most common noun in the Bible used for anger. If this seems to us at first a bit bizarre, we should realize that these words are describing the physical appearance of people who are visibly angry: they turn red and begin to breathe heavily.

In general, the Bible focuses more on the external aspects of an attitude than on the inner states of a person, more on behavior than on feelings. This is even truer in the case of God. So, for example, when the inspired author says that "God remembered his people," he does not intend to claim that something is happening inside God's head, so to speak. He means that God is preparing to act in favor of his faithful, for example by saving them from misfortune by means of concrete acts. Similarly, to say that God gets angry means that there is an outburst of energy from God with destructive consequences. And since human anger is expressed by verbs that evoke breath (wind) and fire, it is understandable that in certain situations a storm or a similar phenomenon would be seen as an expression of "God's wrath."

Let us conclude this chapter by summing up our discoveries. They may seem meager, but they have the advantage of setting us on the right road. First of all, we have realized that the biblical notion of divine wrath is not a mere observation, a raw fact, but rather the interpretation of an experience, understood as an explosion of supernatural energy that has negative consequences. Although such an outburst of energy may well be characteristic of God, its outcome—and therefore the interpretation of the experience as anger—depends to a great extent upon the situation in which this energy is released. For example, the great tempest on Mount Sinai in which the Lord manifested himself when he concluded a covenant with Israel was certainly terrifying:

> When morning came on the third day, there was thunder and lightning, a thick mass of clouds hanging over the mountain and the sound of a powerful trumpet; the entire nation, which was in the camp, trembled. . . . All of Mount Sinai was covered with smoke, since the Lord came down upon it in fire. His smoke billowed up like the smoke of a furnace, and the entire mountain shook violently. (Exod 19:16, 18)

In addition, no one is allowed to approach (19:12–13), since it is sacred ground (19:21–24). Even those who look on from afar have to purify themselves (19:10–11, 22). Just as for Uzza before the ark, it is said: "Anyone who touches the mountain will be put to death" (19:12). There is no question here of anger, however, and the fright of the people, confronted with this manifestation of the divine, should not be confused with fear of punishment. This is rather what will come to be known as "fear of the Lord," a feeling of great awe and wonder in the face of God's otherness, whose ways are not ours (cf. Isa 55:8–9). Here, God's intentions toward those he has brought into the desert are unfailingly good; God has come to make this group of former slaves his own people. And yet the divine presence is inevitably disruptive; it destabilizes and causes a sacred fright. But this is only interpreted as divine wrath when a prohibition is violated or when an obstacle arises and, in that case, when what changes is not the manifestation of God, but the context in which it takes place.

We have also noted in these narratives a tension between the personal and impersonal dimensions. In those long-ago days, the reality of the sacred was largely impersonal; its effects could be compared to a powerful dose of electricity or the explosion of a bomb. Interpreting an event as a manifestation of wrath introduces a personal element, since getting angry is only characteristic of a sentient being. And in that case, what is impersonal may be seen instead as something irrational. To return to the story of Uzza, are we really supposed to imagine that the Creator of the universe loses his temper because a human being reacts without thinking? It is true that, in the ancient texts, this personal dimension is not emphasized: the accent is not placed on the inner life of the one who gets angry, but rather on his or her outward behavior. The biblical theologies of anger, when they attempt to reflect more deeply on God's identity, will find themselves faced with a dilemma hard to resolve—the relationship between this personal God and manifestations which seem to be irrational.

In any event, the notion of divine wrath witnesses to a basic incompatibility between the world as it is, notably the human condition, and the being of God. When God enters the world something is inevitably turned upside down, and certain things are unable to resist. There are things which are apparently incompatible with divine holiness. This observation opens a way forward to a deepening of our topic. Before setting out on that road, however, we need to make a detour by examining more closely the reality of human anger, in the Bible and in itself.

CHAPTER II

Understanding Human Anger

To GAIN A BETTER appreciation of the meaning of anger when applied to God, we must now deepen our understanding of human anger. What causes, in human beings, that explosion of negative energy that we call anger? Does it have a purpose; does it achieve anything? To these questions can be added another one, not less fundamental: how did people in biblical times experience and understand this reality?

Although the reaction of anger is rooted in the biological makeup of human beings and thus has a universal dimension, it expresses itself differently in different times and places. There are variations of temperament that play a role: we all know people who are hotheaded and lose their temper at the least provocation, and others who are unemotional and rarely upset. To these differences can be added those that come from one's upbringing. But the greatest variation in the expression of irritation is certainly cultural. Each civilization tolerates certain forms of behavior and proscribes others, either absolutely or according to the situation or social status of the person concerned. For example, in a given society men may be allowed to express their anger but not women, or else people may be permitted to lose their temper at home but not in public. Before looking at the meaning of human anger in itself, then, let us begin by examining the shape of anger in the world of the Bible.

The Wrath of the King

In a detailed study of human and divine anger in the Bible,[1] the author comes to the conclusion that, in the ancient world as reflected in the biblical writings, anger is expressed almost exclusively by individuals possessing authority, either political (notably the king) or familial (the father, head of the household). They express their anger above all to affirm their authority in a situation where it has been called into question or held in contempt. In a hierarchical society, there was obviously little room for an inferior to show openly his or her exasperation at a superior. The annoyance of those at the bottom of the social hierarchy either had to be repressed or else expressed indirectly: we should note that the text of 2 Samuel 6 mentioned in the previous chapter avoids saying that David's anger at the death of Uzza was specifically directed against the Lord.

This study further notes that, as opposed to hatred, which is by definition lasting and often has fatal results, anger is short-lived. Its consequences are different according to the individual or group at which it is aimed. Directed against the members of one's family—and family bonds in traditional societies were often very broad—anger is usually benign; it rarely leads to harmful acts and often remains on the level of a simple threat. It has a quality that can be characterized as rhetorical—in other words, it is a language used to remind someone of lesser rank of their place in the hierarchy and to confirm the supremacy of the leader. Its aim is therefore to restore correct relationships between people, according to the self-understanding of the society in question. When Rachel, Jacob's wife, accuses her husband of failing to provide her with children, he loses his temper:

> Jacob grew angry at Rachel and said, "Do you take me for God? He is the one who has kept your womb barren!" (Gen 30:2)

But there are apparently no further consequences of this outburst of anger.

---

1. Grant, *Divine Anger.*

The situation of King Saul and his son Jonathan is more dramatic. Saul gets upset with his son because he suspects him of having taken the side of David, whom he considers an enemy. Moreover, since the king is unstable, his rage, even when directed against a close member of his family, runs the risk of ending badly:

> Saul grew angry at Jonathan and said to him, "You son of a perverse and rebellious woman! Don't I know that you are taking the side of the son of Jesse, to your shame! . . . Now get him and bring him to me, for he deserves death." Jonathan answered his father Saul and said to him, "Why should he be put to death? What has he done?" Saul hurled his spear against him to strike him down. . . . Jonathan got up from the table in a rage. (1 Sam 20:30–34)

If Saul's behavior went beyond the bounds of a normal domestic quarrel, we should note that his son provoked him by defending the man that the king saw as his enemy. At that moment, then, in Saul's mind his son was occupying the place of his adversary. We should also note that Jonathan reacted to his father's wrath by getting angry himself, although he did not express it directly. Uncontrolled anger can lead to anger in return, and this is obviously one of the major limits of its usefulness as a means of social control.

If anger between members of the same family or nation generally has no serious consequences, anger provoked by one's enemies can be dangerous, or even fatal. Since there is nothing to restrain it, losing one's temper against an adversary can even lead to his destruction or else turn into lasting hatred. To take an extreme example from a very ancient story found in the book of Judges, such a reaction can be seen in Samson, who takes revenge on the Philistines for using his wife to trick him:

> Samson went down to Ashkelon and struck down thirty men. He took their clothing and gave it to those who had guessed the riddle. Then, [still] burning with anger, he went back up to his father's house. (Judg 14:19)

The author even attributes this fit of rage to "the spirit of the Lord," as a way of indicating that Samson was possessed temporarily by a superhuman and uncontrollable force.

This brief description of anger in the Bible helps us understand that, even if it is not a premeditated and reasonable form of behavior, it is not merely arbitrary. It possesses a logic of its own, accessible to a sociological analysis. Beyond the explicit intentions of those involved and their psychological motivations, anger that is felt and expressed plays a role in structuring society; it signifies that the relationships between the actors have gone too far off course and attempts to restore a certain balance. It is of course a rudimentary social mechanism, benefitting in the first place those who are on top of the social structure and possess authority: women, children, and slaves do not have the luxury of losing their temper. And yet, this anger has a usefulness that goes beyond that of a simple defense reaction of an individual in the face of a threat.

It is interesting in this respect that, in the prophetic writings, the mention of divine wrath is sometimes linked to the image of God as king. Ezekiel only uses the language of kingship once in his entire book, and it is precisely in the context of anger[2]:

> As sure as I live, says the Lord God, it is with a mighty hand, an outstretched arm and an outpouring of wrath that I will be king over you. (Ezek 20:33)

This chapter is a long diatribe by God, speaking through the prophet, against the people's unfaithfulness to the covenant. Although God is the source of the nation's existence and prosperity, Israel prefers to abandon their benefactor in order to run after false gods. The Lord is thus described as a king whose authority is not recognized and, in this context, the mention of anger is entirely appropriate. Such a threat would not have seemed out of line to the prophet's contemporaries; it is exactly what one would expect from a sovereign whose rights have been flouted.

2. Grant, *Divine Anger*, 81.

The Risks of Repression

In our contemporary world, so highly rationalized, anger plays almost no overt role in structuring society. The only exceptions are certain sporadic collective phenomena, such as a spontaneous strike or a public demonstration, those rare moments when a mass of people react unexpectedly against a situation of perceived injustice and grasp the means at hand to express their disagreement. Recently, such manifestations have taken place in the Middle East as part of the so-called Arab Spring, in the United States as a result of police violence against young African-Americans, or, more recently, in the "yellow vests" movement in France. In all such cases, organized groups quickly attempt to canalize such spontaneous expressions of anger and to use them for their own particular ends. In any event, the more rationalized a society becomes, distancing itself from its roots in life and following abstract norms of efficiency and objectivity, the less room there is for expressions of "social anger" to play a positive role. The same thing is true in authoritarian societies, where the only people who can express themselves freely are those who hold power. Is it only by chance that, in our day, virtually the only expressions of anger in a social context are mass murders, where an individual who is at the end of his rope, or a group which is totally opposed to the direction in which society is heading, attempt to blindly eliminate as many of their fellow citizens as possible? It is as if the only possibility they can imagine of using their anger to allow themselves to be heard is an extreme form of acting-out, with consequences that are exclusively negative and destructive.

This situation explains to a great extent our current attitude towards anger and, more specifically, why any mention of this notion to describe God's attitude seems totally outlandish to many. To say it once again, the more rationalized a society becomes, the more a spontaneous and apparently unregulated, or at least nonrational, expression of energy is viewed as unacceptable. This can be seen in Europe, for example, by comparing the character of people in the Mediterranean countries with those from the North of the continent. In the nations that are less "advanced" according to industrial and technological criteria, losing one's temper is part of daily life. Because such behavior is tolerated, it tends to be short-lived and finally of minor significance. The storm breaks and, a few minutes or hours later, the clouds disappear and the sun begins to shine once again.

In the Northern countries, however, expressing one's anger is not considered civilized behavior and, as a result, it often gives rise to feelings of guilt. But since individuals can scarcely refrain from all the feelings of irritation and frustration that are the inevitable counterpart to life with others, they tend to repress their anger and even to hide it from themselves. This repression, although it may lend a certain superficial harmony to life in society, does not offer a real solution. It often leaves problems unresolved and creates unease within people. How many heart attacks and tumors, how much overeating and other forms of addiction in affluent countries are due to energies of life that have been harshly repressed? Would it not be better, instead of denying the reality of anger, to accept that it is part of life and to look for ways of using it in an acceptable fashion, as constructively as possible?

For human anger, left to itself, always entails the danger of violence against persons. If, in less developed cultures, such violence can be observed more overtly in the events of day-to-day life, even within families, more rationalized societies for their part do not escape its ravages. "Cold" forms of violence, ones which are not openly expressed, create just as much damage, and when feelings of rage held back for a long time finally surface, the consequences can be extremely disastrous. In the final analysis, the only efficacious remedy against such violence lies in developing other dimensions of existence, above all relationships of solidarity and empathy between people. When I view others as alter egos, another me, the perils of uncontrolled anger are reduced. In short, the denial of anger and the refusal to take into account its possible positive role in human life do not lead to the well-being of the individual nor to that of society as a whole. By neglecting its emotional bases, human society is in danger of following a downward course towards an existence that is more and more mechanical and less and less human. As we shall see, the anger of the prophets of Israel at a nation cut off from its roots in God was often the last hope for the nation, and an eloquent though uncomfortable sign of God's faithfulness to his wayward people.

Expressing the No[3]

To achieve a correct evaluation of the phenomenon of human anger, one that takes into account both its constructive role and its possible deviations, we must now examine more closely its origins and its physiology. According to the neurobiologists, reactions of anger do not arise in the most developed part of the brain, namely the cortex, but in its most primitive parts. It has become customary in certain circles to speak of the "lizard brain" that ensures the survival of the organism, an organ that we share even with birds and reptiles. Although today, the theory that the human brain is made up of three more or less independent strata which appeared successively in the course of evolution is increasingly called into question in favor of a more complex and interactive model of the brain, it is still plausible that anger belongs to those "primitive" or "instinctive" levels of cerebral functioning that can be called prerational. This may explain the shame that civilized men and women feel after losing their temper.

Prerational, however, is not the same as irrational and, upon closer examination, these instinctive reactions possess their own logic. The survival of the individual, and still more of the group, is a necessity of the first order for living beings. In the face of a per-ceived danger, the ability of an organism to mobilize its energies rapidly and efficiently has an obvious evolutionary advantage. In order to survive, one must quickly react by resisting or by running away, by "fight or flight." This is shown outwardly by changes in the cardiovascular, endocrine, and respiratory systems ("fire and wind") and inwardly by feelings of fear or anger.

3. When it is used in these pages as a technical term to refer to the essence of anger, the word NO (and by contrast YES) is set in small capitals.

To be fully human, however, such reactions must be integrated with the rest of life. In our highly organized societies, it is rare that we are required to flee from our enemies or fight with them. Most of the time, our anger is not aroused by life-or-death situations, but instead by more trivial events that cause our wishes to be frustrated. And in that case, the more developed parts of our intelligence have a role to play, enabling us to modify our instinctive reactions. Is the irritation I feel justified? Should I act upon it and, if so, how? If we dismiss the conviction that anger is inherently negative, the field lies wide open for an evaluation of the appropriateness of our indisposition in each specific case. Should I listen to the irritation that I feel? Is it trying to tell me something about the relationship or the situation I am dealing with, or am I the one who needs to change my perception of reality? Depending upon my answers to these questions, the anger I feel will lead me to a different course of action.

Seen as a global phenomenon, anger can in fact be described as a transcription in one's entire being of the simple word NO. A fit of anger is a blunt refusal in the face of something that demands entry into my existence. This "something" can be as insignificant as the spinach that a child refuses to eat, or as momentous as the racist ideology proclaimed by a fascist regime. In both cases, expressing anger is a way of affirming that a given reality is unacceptable; it has no place in my personal universe.

Viewed in this way, it becomes clear that such a reaction is not necessarily incoherent. In the world as it is, NO is part of our mental equipment. Saying YES to everything and everyone that comes our way would quickly lead to the loss of our identity, and perhaps even of our life. What we call personality or character is formed from our likes and dislikes; it takes its specific form on the basis of elements to which we say NO and others to which we say YES. It is a well-known fact that, as part of normal development, every child goes through a stage when it says NO to practically everything that it is offered. While this behavior is generally trying for the parents, it is essential for the child, so that it can learn how to choose between the alternatives that life proposes. Learning how to say NO is vital so that, later on, a person can establish priorities in their existence and create a scale of values.

If we define anger as the physical and mental expression of a NO to something that lies before me and that asks to be welcomed into my existence, then we can understand that the real question is not "Is it legitimate to get angry?" but rather "What makes me angry, and why?" and then, just as importantly, "What will I do with this anger? How can I use it constructively?" There is a great difference, for example, between someone who loses their temper each time their personal wishes have been frustrated, and someone who gets angry at the injustices in the world, at the exploitation of the weak and the helpless. In the same way, feelings of anger can be expressed by physical or verbal violence, or instead lead a person to act efficaciously to remedy the causes of their frustration. For many people committed to the struggle against injustice, anger is a powerful motivation, necessary if not sufficient. It is the other side of a solidarity with the victims of oppression and of a thirst for a society where justice reigns. As long as the NO does not fill all one's inner space so that it stifles the YES, it can mobilize the energies of the organism to make possible a YES that does not just remain a pious wish.

A Capital Sin?

As a matter of fact, this way of looking at anger is in harmony with the biblical and Christian tradition. For the Bible, as we have seen, anger is part of life. What is deplored, however, is someone who has a "quick temper" (Prov 14:17, 29; 15:18; 22:24; cf. 29:22), who is hot-headed—in other words, someone stuck in an attitude of NO, unable to control their ire. The wise person, in contrast, is "slow to anger" (Prov 14:29; 15:18; 16:32), capable of "a soft answer" (15:1) and self-control (16:32), someone who knows how to avoid quarrels. The Letter of James, a New Testament book very close to the wisdom literature of Israel, likewise recommends being "slow to anger, for a man's anger does not accomplish divine justice" (Jas 1:19–20). James is obviously speaking here of an unreflective, explosive rage, although on a deeper level, it can certainly be helpful to realize that what makes us angry and how we respond may not necessarily be in harmony with the way God sees things. Finally, the Letter to the Ephesians warns against a fit of anger that lasts and runs the risk of turning into hatred and conflict, and advises believers to deal quickly with a situation that triggers a negative reaction:

> Get angry but do not sin. The sun should not set on what provokes you; do not give the devil any room to act. (Eph 4:26–27)

In the Christian era, anger was listed as one of the seven capital or deadly sins, those which lie at the root of many others. But here too, it is important to make the appropriate distinctions. Saint Thomas Aquinas, in his *Summa Theologiae* (IIa–IIae, q. 158), provides an in-depth analysis of anger based on Aristotelian categories. For him, anger is a passion of the sensitive appetite and, in itself, is neither bad nor good. When it is not ruled by right reason, it becomes bad. And it can be so in two ways, first of all because of its object: if it arises from jealousy or envy of others, if it only serves to reinforce our selfishness, then it is blameworthy. And secondly, it can be bad according to its quantity—in other words, when it is expressed in a manner out of proportion to its cause.

The "sensitive appetite" of Saint Thomas corresponds to what we have called the prerational character of anger. It comes from the deeper levels of our being, which are neither rational nor irrational, and it is the use which one makes of it, according to our capacities of intelligence and discernment, that give anger its good or bad quality. Getting angry each time one's own desires or interests are frustrated, losing one's temper over the slightest inconvenience, expressing one's displeasure by a fit of rage out of all proportion to the gravity of the situation. . . all that is part of the capital sin of anger.

Following the thinking of Aristotle, for whom a virtue is always the golden mean between two extremes, Thomas then asks whether there is a vice opposed to anger. Our first impression would probably be to feel that a person can never be too nice or too calm. Well, says our theologian, that is not the case. And he quotes Saint John Chrysostom, who speaks of "unreasonable patience." The humanity of someone who never loses their equanimity on any occasion at all, even in the face of the most glaring injustices, seems to be lacking an essential dimension. If, while walking down the street, I encounter a man violently beating a small child and I go on my way while remaining cool and collected, I am not acting virtuously. What I do with my anger is obviously a further question.

We can ask ourselves whether this last deficiency, namely the inability to feel and to show a righteous anger, is not a particularly widespread failing in our contemporary world. It often appears where anger is seen as inherently negative. Expressed in terms of YES and NO, such a character trait is expressed by the inability to say NO, to set healthy boundaries. Do we not all know parents who feel it would be an intolerable act of violence to refuse their children anything at all? Or people who are always ready to find excuses to justify the most outrageous behavior? Although it may seem paradoxical but is in reality quite understandable, it is not rare for such permissiveness to flip over suddenly and turn into its opposite, a mindless intolerance, fixing upon a certain type of behavior which is then violently attacked and rejected out of hand. It is child's play for the mass media today to whip up the public's fury against a particular head of state, who becomes the latest incarnation of Hitler or Stalin. Once again, where a human reality, here anger, is denied and banned from our consciousness, it tends to go underground and then to surface in the most aggressive and unhealthy forms. It would be far better to recognize it and attempt to integrate it into the whole of our existence.

A Dangerous or Constructive Reaction?

This rapid examination of anger in the Bible and in its essence should allow us to better understand the use of this notion to describe the activity of God. First of all if, long ago, people imagined the deity as a king or the patriarch of a large family, it would be seen as perfectly normal to attribute to him feelings of anger, should his authority be called into question. Fearing God's wrath if his views were not taken into consideration would go without saying, otherwise God would not have seemed to be a serious leader; he would have been a negligent parent.

That does not mean that Israel defined God above all by his irritability, as some people apparently still imagine. On the contrary, as we shall see, at the heart of God's identity is the conviction that God is "slow to anger" (Exod 34:6, etc.), exactly like the wise men and women described in the book of Proverbs. God does not lose his temper easily, so to speak, but always shows patience and great kindness. Nonetheless, for the mentality of the time, forbidding God ever to express discontent as a way of warning his partner of unfaithfulness to the covenant would have implied the absence of any moral and political order in society. The import of this argument should not be misunderstood: I am not attempting here to justify in itself the metaphor of anger applied to God, and still less to claim that this is the best way of describing God's identity and activity. At this stage in our reflections, the important thing is simply to understand that, although the scriptural passages where God seems to get angry may well be a problem for us, this was not necessarily the case in biblical times. Believers in the ancient world could question the justification for an angry reaction in this or that particular situation, or the degree of violence manifested or threatened, but it would have seemed to them unthinkable to deny God any recourse to anger. To do so would mean that the current state of the world was already fully in harmony with the will of its Creator.

Our investigation of the meaning of anger, incidentally, confirms this conclusion. Anger is part of human life and, in this respect, it is not reprehensible; it has a role to play. Nonetheless, like many other elements in our makeup, it must find its place in our existence as a whole. As a source of powerful energy it can be dangerous and destructive but, if it is correctly situated, it can assist the healthy development of the individual and of society. When this energy is denied or turned against itself, it leads to depression, passivity, and even self-destruction. Accepted and channeled, it provides a strong impulse to go forward.

We have also attempted to define the essential quality of anger by the simple word NO, a NO expressed by the entire being when confronted by a reality that wants to be accepted by us and which seems to us inacceptable. In consequence, asking if there is room for anger in God is equivalent to the question: "Are there things to which God says NO?" Formulated in that way, the question can have only one answer. The God of the Bible, precisely because he is goodness and the source of life, cannot say YES to anything that damages or destroys life—contempt, abuse, oppression, torture, cruelty, and so on. God sets limits, creating and maintaining the boundaries that define an authentic life. In this context, the Bible sometimes calls upon the vocabulary of anger.

If our contemporaries have so much difficulty in understanding this dimension of God, is the problem only with the biblical outlook? Could it not testify as well to a deficiency in our contemporary mindset? Are we not threatened by a caricature of love that does not take into account the complexity and the fullness of human existence, a love that remains sentimental and therefore has no real impact on life? People who work with addicts or with those suffering from character disorders sometimes speak of the need for "tough love." Although kindness, tenderness, and forgiveness are essential aspects of loving, they are not sufficient when dealing with deeply wounded individuals who have not received a sound upbringing and who have never learned to set healthy limits to their behavior. In this situation, love also requires firmness, a kind but resolute NO that completes the underlying YES—and one which will not always be appreciated in the short run by the person who hears it. In a word, true love sometimes has a pedagogical dimension. And from a certain point of view, the Hebrew Bible is nothing else than a vast pedagogy by which God leads human beings towards the ability to be worthy partners, preparing them to enter into a true and lasting communion.

After this detour which has enabled us to comprehend human anger a bit better, we shall now return to our investigation of the biblical theologies of anger. We have already noted a tension in the biblical accounts between the personal and the impersonal dimensions. On the one hand, the notion of anger applied to God is an anthropomorphism; it projects a human and therefore personal form of behavior onto the divine. At the same time, God's "wrath" is manifested through impersonal phenomena—a tempest, defeat in a battle, etc. We shall see that these two dimensions give rise to two sorts of theology of divine anger. Let us now examine each of them in turn.

CHAPTER III

Prophetic Anger

WE HAVE SEEN THAT, in archaic civilizations, the domain of the sacred was characterized by a supernatural energy, sometimes explosive, that could have negative consequences in its encounter with the profane world. The God of the Hebrew Bible, like so many other deities in antiquity, was often manifested in phenomena such as a storm or an earthquake. Moreover, certain significant events, for example an unexpected victory in a battle, were likewise attributed to the power of God.

At the same time, to describe these supernatural beings, invisible and mysterious, what other possibility existed than to borrow images from life on earth, and even from human existence? The God of the Bible, because he defended his people and wanted to ensure a felicitous existence for them, was thus often seen as a king. And since kings at that time tended to grow angry when their authority was called into question, as a way of ensuring respect, it was not surprising that this image would also be applied to God.

These two lines merge in the portrait of the God of Israel. First of all, believers could interpret, after the fact, an event such as a military defeat or a natural disaster as an expression of God's wrath as a result of the nation's unfaithfulness. Such an interpretation had the advantage of providing an explanation for realities which otherwise would have remained enigmatic and troubling. The process could also be inverted, with the threat of possible divine anger being used to urge people to repent of behavior that did not correspond to God's wishes. This second possibility likewise offered an advantage on the level of explanation. The obviously harmful consequences for a society of the lack of solidarity and justice are given a kind of personal dimension—they are the expression of the discontent of the Creator of the universe and the Father of his people Israel.

Amos

Those beings of fire whom we call the prophets show best, by their very existence, the link between historical events and the world seen through God's eyes. Far from being fanatics or soothsayers predicting the future, the great prophets of Israel were ordinary men who received a call: God entered their life and sent them as bearers of a message he wanted to address to his people through them. And since God's word passed through their human consciousness, they became unique witnesses of the relationship between the exterior and apparently impersonal face of the world and the activity of a personal God, who lies hidden behind events while directing their course.

The oldest of the prophetic books is that written by Amos, a herdsman in the southern kingdom during the eighth century before the Common Era. He was taken by the Lord "from behind his flocks" and sent to the royal sanctuary of Bethel in the northern kingdom, at the other end of the country, to speak in God's name (Amos 7:14–15). With his eyes enlightened by God, Amos sees, behind its façade of apparent peace and prosperity, a society which is seriously ill. Having forgotten the source of its life, the relationship with a liberating God, this society is being undermined by the selfish quest for individual well-being and the growing division between rich and poor resulting from this. With no indulgence, the prophet exposes the symptoms of this illness and evokes the consequences that will not fail to follow from it. One passage can serve as an example:

> Hear this, you who trample on the needy
> to exterminate the lowly of the land, saying:
> "When will the New Moon be over
> so we can sell our grain,
> and the Sabbath, so we can offer our wheat for sale,
> reducing the ephah-measure, increasing the shekel,
> cheating with dishonest scales,
> ruining the poor for money
> and the needy for a pair of sandals?
> We will even sell the sweepings of the grain!"
> The Lord swears by the Pride of Jacob:
> I will never forget a single deed of theirs!
> Is this not why the earth will quake
> and all its inhabitants be in mourning?
> It will rise up like the great River
> and toss and turn like the Nile.
> (Amos 8:4–8)

The catastrophe that Amos sees looming on the horizon, the ineluctable result of the nation's iniquity, is described by means of various images—a natural disaster (cf. Amos 1:2; 8:8; 9:5), a conflagration (1:4, 7, 10, 12, 14; 2:2, 5; 5:6; 7:4), a military defeat (2:15; 5:5, 27; 6:7; 7:17; 9:10). But most often, the termination of Israel's hopes remains undefined; it is simply the Lord's passing in their midst that will put an end to injustice (3:14; 4:12; 5:17). Here we have the theme of the "Day of the Lord," destined to have such a prolific future in the preaching of the prophets. At first, this "day" referred to a favorable event, the Lord's intervention to save his beleaguered people just as he did for their ancestors in Egypt centuries earlier. But the originality of our prophet is that he thwarts the popular expectation, which relied on the notion of a "chosen people" as an unconditional guarantee enabling them to act with impunity. The nation's faith was well on its way to deluding itself with what the German theologian Dietrich Bonhoeffer would call many centuries later "cheap grace," a love with no exigencies. In the language of the previous chapter, it is a question of a YES that does not integrate the dimension of the NO. Confronted by this reduction of divine love, Amos speaks out boldly:

Alas for those longing for the Day of the Lord!
Why do you want it to arrive?
For you the Day of the Lord will be darkness, not light. . . .
Will it not be dark, the Day of the Lord, and not bright,
bleak and gloomy, without a ray of light?
(5:18, 20)

In other words, God's prevenient love cannot be captured for a human cause. Used to justify behavior in contradiction to divine justice, this energy turns back against those who believe they possess it. It explodes their achievements and sets them before a void.

Although Amos underlines the destructive activity of a God who disabuses false certainties, for his part he never uses the language of anger. It is as if the vision he has of God is too lofty to allow him to go very far in personalizing the divinity. He does not dare to venture very far into the inscrutable regions of divine psychology, preferring instead images taken from nature: the God of Israel is for him like a roaring lion (1:2; 3:8, 12), or a bear (5:19), or more generally an implacable force. It is true that God speaks (3:7–8) and leads his people (2:10); Amos even says that God "hates" the hypocritical worship of Israel (5:21) and its fortresses (6:8). But all that is an attempt to describe God's activity rather than to analyze God's inner life. For this prophet God remains the Creator, the "God of [the heavenly] hosts" (*YHWH Tsebaoth*, 3:13; 4:13; 5:14–16, 27; 6:8, 14), who is above everything (4:13; 5:8; 9:6) and who is not accountable to anyone. In other words, for Amos God, the guardian of a moral order embodied in his covenant with Israel, makes sure that no attempt to create another "order" contrary to his justice remains standing. If the unfathomable God communicates his designs to the prophets (3:7; cf. 4:13), that is above all in order to warn the nation so that it may perhaps change its behavior (5:14–15), not in order to reveal his inner life.

Isaiah

If, for the prophet Amos, the notion of divine anger remains implicit, his successor, the great Isaiah of Jerusalem, who comes upon the stage of history a few years later, goes a step further than his predecessor. Isaiah has a similarly exalted vision of God, "the Holy One of Israel" whom he encountered in a life-changing experience in the temple of Jerusalem at the beginning of his ministry (Isa 6). Like Amos, Isaiah realizes that God hates worship that does not go hand in hand with the endeavor to do what is right (1:10–18). And just as for his predecessor, the day of the Lord offers for this prophet no false consolation (2:6–22). That day will be primarily a revelation of "the splendor of his majesty" (2:19, 21), when "all that is proud, haughty and exalted" will be cast down (2:12), when all human pride that puffs itself up at the expense of God and others will be shown to be ludicrous. In this context, Isaiah employs the notion of "terrifying, causing to tremble" with a nice play on words almost impossible to render in English. Everyone will hide themselves

> before the dread of the Lord
> and the splendor of his majesty
> when he will rise up to terrify the terrestrial (the earth)
> (*la'arots ha'arets*).
> (2:19, 21)

But here too, these words describe less the attitude of the Lord than the effect of his majesty on human beings who cling to their fictions. It is the contrast that is emphasized: in the face of the absolute Reality that is God, the pretensions of human beings evaporate like the morning mist at the rising of the sun.

Unlike Amos, however, Isaiah does not hesitate to use the vocabulary of anger to describe the present and future activity of God. His wrath can be directed against his people, when they flout his edicts of justice and solidarity. In a long and ironic poem that opposes the repeated unfaithfulness of the nation to God's faithfulness to his designs, the same refrain is taken up again and again:

> But for all that his anger did not cease
> and his hand is still stretched out.
> (5:25; 9:11, 16, 20; 10:4)

In other words, God is not satisfied with half-measures, but demands a sincere and lasting change of heart.

The Holy One of Israel is even able to make use of foreign nations to accomplish his designs. In this sense, speaking through the prophet, God calls Assyria, the great power that is in the process of conquering the world, "the rod of my anger" (10:5). This inspired interpretation places the activity of a foreign nation under the control of the God of Israel and, by doing so, prevents the people of God from believing that their God is weaker than the gods of Assyria and thus from sinking into despair. Moreover, if the Lord's anger indeed lies hidden behind the activity of Assyria, then a door for hope can open:

> And so, thus says the Lord God of hosts:
> O my people who dwell in Zion,
> do not fear Assyria, who strikes you with the rod
> and raises its stick against you as Egypt did,
> for in a very little while my fury will be spent
> and my anger will turn to their destruction.
> (10:24–25)

As a matter of fact, the rage of the King (6:5) against his subjects will not last forever. The stick will be followed by the carrot, when the Lord will once again show his face of compassion (14:1):

> You will say on that day:
> I praise you, O Lord,
> for you were angry with me
> but your anger ceased and you comfort me. (12:1)

God's wrath against his people, fearsome as it may be, is thus never the last word. In the case of foreign nations, however, the situation is not the same. As with personal anger against one's enemies, God's anger against the adversaries of Israel has no inherent limits (cf. 30:27–33; 34:2). The day will dawn when all the forces of evil—in other words, all that keeps the faithful from living in *shalom* (peace, well-being, prosperity, etc.)—will be eliminated once and for all. In the Isaian oracles that evoke this situation, divine wrath against the nations tends to be identified with the day of the

Lord, when God will reveal his incomparable majesty, as he did on Sinai, "with thunder and trembling and the great noise of a gale, a tempest and the flame of a devouring fire" (29:6). On that day, all the pretensions of human beings to establish their own justice by exalting themselves will be brought to nothing:

> See, the Day of the Lord is coming,
> ruthless and overflowing with burning anger
> to reduce the land to ruin
> and exterminate its sinners.
> The stars of the sky and their constellations
> will no longer give light.
> The sun at its rising will be dark
> and the moon will not shine.
> I will visit evil upon the world
> and upon the wicked their iniquity.
> I will remove the pride of the insolent
> and abase the arrogance of the violent.
> I will make humankind rarer than pure gold,
> rarer than the gold of Ophir.
> That is why I will cause the heavens to quake
> and the earth will waver on its foundations
> because of the fury of the Lord of hosts
> on the day of his burning anger. (13:9–13)

As for those who put their trust in the Lord, all that the prophet can advise them to do is to hide themselves when the Day arrives and to wait until the storm subsides:

> Go, my people, enter your chambers
> and shut the door behind you.
> Hide yourselves for a few moments,
> until the anger passes by,
> for see, the Lord is coming from his dwelling
> to visit their iniquity upon the inhabitants of the earth.
> The earth will disclose its blood
> and no longer hide its victims.
> (26:20–21)

It is evident that this "anger" is primarily an impersonal reality, for, like a natural disaster, it descends upon all without exception.

In conclusion, if Isaiah, unlike Amos, does not hesitate to use the language of anger to describe God's activity when confronted with human injustice, this seems to be a difference of form rather than content. For this prophet, language of this sort is much less an attempt to "personalize" God than a way to describe his actions—an outburst of energy, seen from without, that reduces to ashes all that resists it. The Holy One of Israel is indeed, for him, the King, and thus a being permitted to express his wrath, but he is a King of an utterly different sort than any human sovereign. The modern tendency to imagine a god in the human image, in order to subsequently criticize or reject such a deity, would have been incomprehensible to Isaiah: God is God, and has no need to justify himself before anyone. Speaking of God's anger is simply one more way to affirm that God is the absolute and everlasting Reality, and that those who build their lives on other foundations are heading for disaster.

Hosea and Jeremiah

Alongside these prophets of a "high" and "lofty" God (Isa 57:15), whose ways are inscrutable (cf. Isa 55:8–9), another prophetic tendency arose, represented by Hosea and Jeremiah. Not that these latter prophets had a less exalted vision of God; they were not "liberals" ahead of their time, people who attempted to imprison the Creator of the universe in their own limited categories, clothing him in the psychology of the man in the street. The process went rather in the other direction: God was the one who, in communicating with them, took greater possession of their inner life. As a result, it was their life as much as their words that tended to become a revelation of the divine. With them we are already on the way to the incarnation of the Word, which culminates for Christians in the figure of Christ Jesus, God's Word made flesh (cf. John 1:14). This "humanization" of God would have significant consequences for the theme of anger, revealing both its specific character and its limits.

The first words spoken by God to Hosea, a younger contemporary of Amos, already set us on what we have just referred to as the road of incarnation. The Lord orders him to marry an unfaithful woman, perhaps a prostitute, and to have children with her. In doing so, Hosea becomes a kind of living parable of the relationship between God and Israel, "for the land is behaving just like a prostitute, turning away from the Lord" (Hos 1:2). The Lord became attached to his people with deep affection and lavished gifts on her, but Israel continued to run after her "lovers," ostensibly the fertility gods of Canaan, neglecting her first love. As was the case for other prophets, the unfaithfulness of the human partner causes an outburst of anger in God (8:5); God will take on the persona of a wild beast, a lion or a bear (5:14; 11:10; 13:7–8).

But given the personal history of Hosea, these infrahuman metaphors fade before that of a husband with his adulterous wife. And as a result, the specific character of this anger is revealed. Far from being the result of a difficult temperament or of spontaneous antipathy, it is basically the other side of a spurned love, the mortifying resentment of someone who gave his heart to another, only to find that the beloved responds with indifference or rejection. The threats and expressions of fury, therefore, do not aim at the destruction of the other person; their sole purpose is to try and bring her back to the beautiful relationship that once existed "in the day of her youth, when she came up out of the land of Egypt" (2:17). The rejected lover tries to get the wayward spouse to see that her true happiness is found in this relationship, for it is the source of all that she possesses. By situating the expression of anger within a conjugal relationship, the book of Hosea makes its nature and its link to God's identity clear: this anger is in the final analysis nothing else than the other side of love, the dark side, manifested precisely by its rejection.

The prophet Jeremiah, active in the southern kingdom over a century later, is the one for whom we have the most biographical data and thus, of all the prophets of Israel, the one whose existence best reflects his message. Seemingly a gentle and sensitive man, who feels he has little aptitude for the grim ministry to which God has called him (cf. Jer 1:6), he is forced to prepare his contemporaries for a time when the Lord will "uproot and pull down... destroy and demolish," before being able to "build and plant" once again (1:10). These sets of verbs, incidentally, express wonderfully what we have called the NO and the YES. It is always the same God, whose intentions are infallibly good (cf. 29:11), but depending upon the situation of his partner this goodness can assume radically different forms; false convictions that shield people from the truth have to be uprooted so that a message of solace can be correctly understood.

Like his predecessors, Jeremiah knows and develops the doctrine of God's "external" anger. Like a roaring lion (4:7; 25:30) or a vexed king (10:10), God vents his wrath upon his people (4:8, 26; 7:20; 12:13; 17:4; 21:5, 12). But, in fact, this activity is caused by the misdeeds of Israel, which "does not take into account the order established by the Lord" (8:7; cf. 5:25). The nation remains rebellious (2:30; 5:3), while protesting all the while its innocence (2:35). Certainly, God will not lose his temper forever (3:12), at least against his own people, whereas for the enemies of Israel there are no guarantees (cf. 49:37; 50:13; 51:45). Nonetheless, "the time of anger" is part of God's designs, which is a way of saying that it is not irrational but has a pedagogical intention only able to be understood in retrospect:

> The Lord's anger will not turn away
> until he has accomplished and achieved
> his deepest purpose.
> Later on, you will gain a full understanding of this.
> (23:20; 30:24)

In the end, what God is aiming at is to foster a deep and lasting change in the life of his followers, a radical transformation that Jeremiah calls a "circumcision of the heart" (4:4; 9:25). And then, says God,

> I will gather them from all the lands to which I banished them in my anger, my fury and my great wrath. I will bring them back to this place and cause them to dwell here in security. They will be for me a people, and I will

> be God for them. I will give them one heart and a single
> way, to respect me always, for their good and the good of
> their children after them. I will make an everlasting cov-
> enant with them; I will not cease to do good to them and
> I will put a great awe of me in their hearts, so they will
> never turn away from me. My joy will be to act for their
> benefit, and I will settle them in this land for good. I will
> do this with all my heart, with all my soul. (32:37–41)

In this way Jeremiah continues and prolongs the same line as his predecessors. Anger is seen more and more as an impersonal reality, the inevitable consequence of an inauthentic life. God, for his part, never wavers in his intention to give the fullness of life to those he has called. But this purpose of God's obliges him to take unexpected detours as a result of the response—or lack of re-sponse—of his partners. To those who reject it, love takes the form of a destructive energy, a consuming fire. But what it consumes is everything that keeps human beings from living their vocation to the full. An oracle from a much later prophet shows us, by using the image of fire and heat, how these two realities which are so different for us are in fact one and the same on the side of God:

> See, the Day is coming, ablaze like a furnace. All the ar-
> rogant and all evildoers will be like straw. The Day that
> is coming will set them on fire, says the Lord of hosts,
> leaving neither root nor branch. But for you who fear my
> name, the sun of justice will rise, bringing healing in its
> rays. (Mal 4:1–2)

A consuming fire or a warming sun, then, according to the quality of the receiver. This vision of divine wrath, taken up and systematized by the Deuteronomic school and already visible in the final edition of the book of Jeremiah, will become the most common theology of anger found in the Scriptures, even influenc-ing a number of New Testament texts.

Anger Interiorized

At the same time, alongside this presentation of anger as an external reality, Jeremiah follows Hosea in developing its inner dimension as well. First of all, he takes up the image of Israel as an unfaithful wife and of the Lord as a betrayed husband (Jer 2:2, 20; 3:1–5, 20; 30:14), although this has no parallel in his own existence, since God had ordered him not to marry (16:2). Still, this anger, the other face of love, enters into him and takes possession of his whole being:

> My bowels, my bowels! I writhe in pain!
> The walls of my heart!
> My heart is beating wildly;
> I cannot keep silent. (4:19)

On the one hand, the prophet is "filled with the wrath of the Lord [and is] exhausted at trying to hold it in" (6:11). On the other, he loves his people and understands better than anyone the tragedy of their unfaithfulness. As a result, in addition to the oracles addressed to the nation, the personal life of Jeremiah becomes the site of God's revelation. The prophet lives out the drama of Israel in his own being. Interiorized, the interplay of divine anger and love engenders a terrible inner conflict:

> My grief is incurable, my heart afflicted. . . .
> My people's wound wounds me; I am in mourning;
> horror takes hold of me. . . .
> Who will turn my head into a flood,
> my eyes into a fountain of tears,
> so that I may weep day and night
> for the victims of my people?
> (8:18, 21, 23; cf. 13:17; 14:17)

Torn between the desire to do good to his contemporaries and the need to bring them back to the way of justice, Jeremiah is placed in an impossible situation. His mission sets him apart from his fellows: "under your hand I sit alone, for you have filled me with outrage" (15:17; cf. 16:1–9). For their part they reject him; he is "a man who provokes strife and contention in the whole land"

(15:10): "I have become a laughing-stock the whole day long; everyone makes fun of me. . . . God's word has become for me a source of abuse and derision the whole day long" (20:7–8). Divine inspiration is like a fire burning within him that he cannot hold back (20:9) and that intoxicates him (23:9). Rebuffed by his companions while at the same time seemingly abandoned by his God, the prophet remains alone with his "incurable wound" (10:19; 15:18). Personalized and thus revealed as the reverse side of a love which is scorned, anger leads to an impasse. Apparently destined to hurt and to destroy, in the end it hurts even more deeply the one who feels it, by breaking his heart.

This process was already visible in Hosea, as a result of his relationship with an unfaithful wife described at the beginning of his book, a parable of the link between Israel and the Lord. In this way, transposed onto a human psychology of conjugal life, the struggle within God becomes understandable. Faced with the unfaithfulness of his partner, the husband expresses his deep bitterness: "I will strip her naked. . . . I will uncover her shame. . . . I will stop all her rejoicing. . . . I will lay waste her vines and fig trees" (Hos 2:5–15). But all at once, he realizes that, by doing so, it is his own love that will be wounded, and suddenly the tone changes:

> And so, I will seduce her
> and bring her into the wilderness
> and speak to her heart. . . .
> I will betroth you to me for ever
> I will betroth you to me in righteousness and justice,
> in love and tenderness.
> I will betroth you to me in faithfulness
> and you will know the Lord.
> (2:16, 21–22)

Here it is God who undergoes a transformation, which leaves open the question of how this change can have an effect on the human partner.

The same kind of transformation is expressed later on in the book of Hosea, even more clearly, but this time not by means of the man-woman relationship but through that of father and son. First there is unrequited love, leading to anger:

> When Israel was a youth, I loved him,
> and out of Egypt I called my son.
> The more I called them, the more they turned away from me:
> they sacrificed to the Baals and made offerings to idols.
> And yet I was the one who taught Ephraim to walk
> and took him by the arm.
> But they did not realize that it was I who was taking care of them. . . .
> Assyria will be their king
> because they refused to return to me.
> The sword will whirl through their cities;
> it will put an end to their defenses
> and devour them because of their intrigues.
> (11:1–2, 5–6)

Then all at once, a reversal:

> How can I give you up, Ephraim,
> and hand you over, Israel? . . .
> My heart is overturned within me
> and at the same time my pity is kindled.
> I will not give rein to my burning anger;
> I will not return and destroy Ephraim.
> For I am God and not a human being.
> In your midst I am the Holy One
> and I will not come in wrath.
> (11:8–9)

Harming one's beloved son means hurting oneself even more. It means cutting off one's nose to spite one's face, and so the logic of anger cannot follow its course to the end. Jeremiah seems to follow the same pattern, although it must be admitted that the passage is somewhat obscure and thus the translation is uncertain:

> Is Ephraim not my beloved son,
> the child of my delight,
> so that whenever I remonstrate with him
> I must still remember him [with affection].

That is why my bowels are deeply moved for him.
Indeed I love him, says the Lord.
(Jer 31:20)

In these oracles we see a development similar to the man-woman relationship, namely an expression of indignation at betrayal by the loved one, followed by an awareness of the deep affection that links them whatever may happen, and then a calming of the storm. Anger is transformed by passing through an inner struggle; it turns into suffering and culminates in a renewed and deepened love.

In these two prophets, anger is expressed through human psychology and thus reveals its inner workings. In doing so, it opens up perspectives which are as mind-boggling as they are inexplicable. It reveals a combat and a reversal on the side of God, without it being made clear just how this transformation can affect the situation of the unfaithful people. If anger, seen as a stage in an inner drama, manifests the close link in God between his fury and his affection—the former being in some sense the shadow of the latter—it gives little information for comprehending the effects of this anger on the human partner. That is perhaps why this inner and personalized vision of God's anger remains relatively rare in the Hebrew Scriptures. For the most part, the inspired authors of Israel will remain attached to a theology of divine wrath which is outward or impersonal. It is this theology that we now need to examine, while waiting for a reflection on God's inner life to spring up again with renewed force in the gospel of Jesus of Nazareth.

CHAPTER IV

Explanatory Anger and its Critics

IN OUR READING OF the prophets of Israel, we identified two manifestations of divine anger. A first tendency was objective and external, identifying upheavals of nature or other events as God's response to the misdeeds of the people, or the consequence of these. A second tendency was more subjective and inward: the prophet experienced in his own inner life the divine reaction to the unfaithfulness of those God had called. In this case, anger underwent a transformation. It was revealed for what it in fact is—the reverse of an unconditional love, and this love ended up changing the expression of irritation, by means of an inner struggle, into a renewed and deepened affection.

This latter tendency, although undoubtedly more profound, offered fewer possibilities for explaining events, and for this reason it remained marginal in the Hebrew Scriptures. The former tendency, on the other hand, would enjoy great success in the historical books of the Bible. We have already observed that the notion of anger applied to God is not a raw fact but an interpretation. In the historical books, this phenomenon is taken to the extreme. The editors use the notion as a preferred means to explain events in the life and history of Israel. As a result, divine wrath tends to lose its rootedness in a concrete experience and become a global concept, ultimately even an abstract one. What it thereby gains in explanatory power is counterbalanced by a loss of specificity and relevance to particular cases. At the end of this process, "the wrath of God" becomes in practice little more than a technical term to describe the consequences of evil in a universe which is the handiwork of a Creator who is good and the source of goodness.

The Deuteronomic History

This use of anger as an explanatory category is visible above all in what is generally called *the Deuteronomic history*. Bible scholars of the twentieth century noticed that the books of Joshua, Judges, 1–2 Samuel, and 1–2 Kings presented a great unity of perspective, not on the level of the stories taken individually, which can often be quite ancient and diverse, but on the level of the overall comprehension of the history of God's chosen people. In addition, the main lines of this history echoed certain key themes in the book of Deuteronomy. These observations gave rise to the hypothesis that the final version of these books was the work of a group of editors, sometimes known as "the Deuteronomic school," influenced by that book and continuing its outlook. This hypothesis was subsequently refined, for example by distinguishing at least two different stages, one which went back to the time of King Josiah, when a preliminary version of the book of Deuteronomy was discovered in the temple around 620 BCE (see 2 Kgs 22–23), and another dated after the fall of Jerusalem in 587. The prose sections of the book of the prophet Jeremiah are generally also included in this list of Deuteronomic documents, since their perspective is almost identical.

A text placed at the beginning of the book of Judges, those charismatic and provisional leaders who united and mobilized the proto-Israelite clans in the face of danger during the early years of their settlement in the land of Canaan, already shows us the main lines of the history of Israel as seen through the spectacles of the Deuteronomic school. It is striking to see what extent the theme of anger serves as the linchpin to understand the sequence of events:

> The children of Israel did what was evil in the eyes of
> the Lord and served the Baals. They abandoned the Lord,

the God of their ancestors, who had brought them out of the land of Egypt, and they followed other gods among the gods of the surrounding nations; they worshipped them and made God angry. . . . God's wrath was inflamed against Israel: he handed them over to plunderers who plundered them and sold them to their enemies on all sides. They were not able to resist in the face of their enemies. . . . So the Lord raised up judges who saved them from those who were plundering them. But they did not even listen to their judges. . . . The Lord was with the judge and delivered them from their enemies during the life of the judge, for the Lord was moved by their groaning before their tormentors and oppressors. But when the judge died, they went back to their immoral behavior. . . . The Lord's anger was inflamed against Israel and he said, "Because this nation has violated my covenant, the one I enjoined upon their ancestors, and did not listen to my voice, neither will I continue any longer to dispossess the nations that Joshua left behind." (Judges 2:11–21; cf. 3:7–9; 2 Kgs 13:1–6)

Infidelity of the nation, divine wrath, misfortunes suffered by Israel,[1] repentance of the nation, divine forgiveness and sending of a "savior" (Judg 3:9, 15; 2 Kgs 13, 5)—until the cycle begins once again, apparently without end. This basic structure shows the importance of our topic for understanding the history of salvation. Anger interests the authors not in itself, as a literal description of what may be taking place in God's bosom, so to speak, but as the indispensable link between the Lord and a nation whose existence

---

1. There is a great temptation to use the word "punishment" in this context, all the more so because this reinforces the rationalization of anger, which is then transformed from a spontaneous expression of displeasure into a juridical procedure. We should remember, though, that in the language of the Bible, the verb "to punish" does not exist; the texts speak instead of "visiting" upon people the evil they have committed. For this reason, as well as on account of changing attitudes and the contemporary connotations of this vocabulary (people almost never speak of "punishing" their children or pupils any more), the notion of punishment leads only to confusion. In my opinion, it would be a great step forward if it were used as rarely as possible in biblical and theological language.

is characterized by unfaithfulness. The pair anger/misfortunes serves as the middle term between the deviance of the nation and its return to God. Without this middle term, there would be no continuity in historical events, no history as such, for we would be left only with the dyad "offer of salvation—Israel's refusal." This way of constructing a narrative serves rather to show that God for his part remains faithful, for anger is the opposite of indifference. And the fact that this wrath is expressed by hardships suffered by the nation gives it consistency and the possibility for God's partner to react.

Within this basic scheme we find variations, however, notably concerning the relationship between divine anger and the calamities of Israel. This is determined above all by two necessities. There is first of all the desire to keep the initiative in God's hands, since anger is an expression of divine faithfulness, God's refusal to abandon his people definitively. But at the same time, we find the wish to absolve God from behavior too flagrantly in contradiction with his identity as "the merciful and gracious God, slow to anger" (Exod 34:6). Because of this, the link between the Lord and his wrath tends to become more indirect. The texts depict less a God who loses his temper like a human being and speak of "wrath" as a reality in itself, an instrument or agent of destruction that, while it has its source in God, is not really a direct expression of the divine identity. On the other hand, the relation between the crimes of the people and the consequent disasters tends to become more direct, moving in the direction of what can be called self-destructive behavior: the evil committed by human beings turns back against them by a kind of boomerang effect. In the book of Jeremiah, for example, after an evocation of divine anger, we read:

> And now thus says the Lord, the God of hosts, the God of Israel: Why are you doing such great harm to yourselves, wiping yourselves out—men and women, children and infants—from the midst of Judah, so as not to leave even a remnant behind? Making me angry by the works of your hands, offering sacrifices to other gods here in the land of Egypt where you have come to dwell, wiping

yourselves out and becoming accursed and ridiculed among all the nations of the earth! (Jer 44:7–8)

In other words, "they have run after worthless idols and so have become worthless themselves" (2 Kgs 17:15; cf. Jer 2:5). In these passages, what God does is simply to ratify the sentence that the nation has already pronounced upon itself by its abominable conduct. In this context we sometimes see the verb "to hand over" employed, as in the text from the book of Judges quoted above. Instead of acting directly against evildoers, God "hands them over" to the powers of destruction. In the final analysis, it is the evil committed by human beings that exercises its adverse effects on their lives. When they leave the roads of God, they go astray on dangerous ground that can lead only to perdition.

Innocent, but Condemned

The Deuteronomic theology of divine anger thus serves paradoxically to reinforce the faith of the people of Israel, allowing the nation to undergo the most complete reversals of fortune without losing their trust in the Lord. In this way, the editors of the biblical history could explain even the greatest disaster of the nation's existence, the fall of Jerusalem in 587 BCE and the deportation which followed. Far from being a proof of the powerlessness of the God of Israel or of divine indifference, the calamity was attributed to the sins of the people, beginning with their ruler:

> And yet the Lord did not return from the burning of his great wrath which flared up against Judah, because of all the ways in which Manasseh provoked him to anger. The Lord said: Judah too I will remove from before my face, just as I removed Israel. I will reject this city which I chose, Jerusalem, and the House of which I said, my Name will be there. (2 Kgs 23:26–27; cf. 21:2–15; 22:15–17)

According to this vision of things, God remains the Lord of history and thus a new beginning is always possible, if human beings only repent and turn back to their Maker. Despite its obvious advantages, such a theology remains extremely fragile. Easy to caricature, it can slide towards a moralistic and idealistic outlook, where good is always rewarded and evil punished. It is sometimes criticized nowadays as a flagrant example of "blaming the victim," by implicitly affirming that she deserved the misfortunes she is suffering. Already in the Scriptures, this way of understanding things is far from enjoying general acceptance. First and foremost, it comes up against the common experience of ordinary people, who know that those who are faithful to God do not always enjoy a good life, whereas those who turn their backs on him often seem to flourish.

This theme of the suffering of the righteous and the prosperity of the wicked is particularly visible in the book of Psalms. Many of these liturgical chants are calls for help in which the protagonist, who sees himself as someone afflicted and oppressed (*'ani,* Ps 10:9, 12; 34:6; 35:10; *'anah,* Ps 10:17; 22:26; *'ebyon,* 140:12), implores the Lord to save him from his powerful adversaries. "How long will my enemy prevail over me? Look, answer me, Lord my God!" (Ps 13:2–3); "Hear the voice of my pleading when I cry to you for help" (28:2); "Assail those who assail me, O Lord; fight those who fight me" (35:1); "O God, do not keep silent; do not remain passive and quiet, O God. See, your enemies are in uproar; those who hate you are lifting up their heads" (83:1–2). Here we find ourselves in a universe where the violent and the dishonest seem to be in charge, while God's friends are at a loss. It is true that these psalms do express trust in a God who is disposed to act in order to change things; they sometimes even end with words of thanksgiving for the liberation received. Nonetheless, they show clearly that a vision of the world where suffering is the result of unfaithfulness to God does not correspond to the lived reality of many individuals.

One biblical prayer deals directly with this problem, Psalm 73. The psalmist explains that he was envious of the happiness of the proud and arrogant, which almost caused him to lose his faith in God. *Why should I remain faithful?* he thought. "I have kept my heart pure in vain" (v. 13). At the end of a difficult period of questioning, he finally discovers the key to the enigma. The happiness of the wicked is only temporary, he realizes, and in the end they will come to nothing, whereas those who do right will always be with the Lord:

> With you there is nothing I desire on earth.
> My flesh and my heart are wasted
> but God is the support of my heart and my portion for ever.
> (Ps 73:25–26)

Psalms 37 and 49 continue this same line of thinking. (Human) anger against the wicked is futile because, in any event, their success is short-lived. "They will quickly dry up like the leaves and wither like the green grass" (Ps 37:2). For believers, the main thing is to "trust in the Lord and do good" (v. 3), to "keep quiet with the Lord and hope patiently in him" (v. 7), to "wait for the Lord and remain on his path" (v. 34). It should be noticed that with this outlook we leave behind a simple affirmation of the misfortune of the wicked and the happiness of the righteous here and now. The solution to the problem lies in shifting to another level. If the faithful are happy now, that is because they trust in the Lord and hope in him, even if the present circumstances of their lives are hard. Psalm 49 even locates this change of situation at death. The evildoer may imagine that his good fortune will last forever, but he will end up in the Pit:

> For in dying, he takes nothing with him;
> all his glory does not go down with him. . . .
> They will go to join their ancestors
> and never again see the light. (Ps 49:17, 19)

The faithful, on the other hand, possess an indefectible hope: "God will ransom my life from the power of Sheol; yes, he will take care of me" (v. 15). In these psalms, God's wrath, with its short-term consequences, gives way to larger perspectives: the enigma of the suffering of the innocent is only finally solved by exiting from this world towards the world of God—and God's world, accessible here and now through faith and hope, can make our present life bearable in spite of all its setbacks.

Other biblical books likewise call into question a facile theology of happiness and unhappiness. Qoheleth, a late book of wisdom supposedly from the pen of the great King Solomon, disparages this outlook in the name of experience, in a tone of voice that often comes close to cynicism:

> I have seen everything in my meaningless life:
> a righteous person perishing while doing good,
> a wicked person living a long life while doing evil.
> (Qoh 7:15; cf. 8:10–14; 9:2)

This teacher of wisdom does not advocate moral relativism, however. He knows that "God will judge the good and the evil" (Qoh 3:17; cf. 11:9; 12:13), even if "all comes from dust and all returns to dust" (3:20). The wisest thing we can do, then, while we are still on this earth, is to avoid extremes (cf. 7:16–17) and enjoy the simple pleasures that life offers (cf. 2:24; 3:22; 5:17; 8:15; 9:7–10).

When it comes to criticism of the prevailing theology, however, the place of honor must be accorded to the book of Job. "An upright and honest man, who feared God and avoided evil" (Job 1:1), Job ends up suffering in every way possible. In his utter distress, he attempts to comprehend what has brought him to this pass. Since the modern facile solution, postulating a universe which is simply absurd, is inconceivable to him, he is forced to assume that God is the source of his misery: "Who of them all does not know that the Lord's hand has done this? His anger is kindled against me and he treats me as an enemy" (12:9; 19:11). In an attempt to console him, his friends lay out all the traditional explanations for his misfortune. It is the wicked who end up badly (4:7–9; 15:20–35; 18:5–21; 20:4–29), they explain to him, and therefore you must be guilty; if you return to God all will go well with you (ch. 22). Job, however, continues to proclaim that he is innocent (27:5–6), even though he knows that he has no hope of prevailing over God (9:20). He also is aware that it is often the enemies of God who prosper (ch. 21). Continuing to resist the arguments of his friends, he keeps alive a faint hope (19:25–27) in the face of a God who seems perverse.

The book of Job thus presents with great clarity the limits of the Deuteronomic theology in offering a coherent vision of the moral character of the universe created by God. Although we know very little about the background of the book, some scholars conjecture that it was written shortly after the fall of Jerusalem and the exile in Babylon to dispute the traditional explanation of the catastrophe. The book shows well the problems with the conventional vision, but it must be admitted that it does not offer a fully satisfactory alternative. At the end of the book, God speaks in the first person. By offering the unfortunate victim a more direct and deeper experience of the divinity, God causes Job to realize that he cannot argue with God as an equal, since he lacks some essential information; however hard he may try, Job will never be able to see things from the divine point of view. At the same time, the arguments of Job's companions are clearly rejected by God as insufficient and even worthy of condemnation. He says to Eliphaz, "I am burning with anger against you and your two friends, for you did not speak of me truly, as did my servant Job" (42:7). And Job sees his previous situation restored and even improved. As a criticism of the reigning theology and an invitation to examine things more deeply, the book of Job is unrivaled, but in the final analysis it leaves us unsatisfied. Where is this "redeemer" Job is longing for with all his strength? Surprisingly, it is an unbeliever, one often contemptuous of traditional faith, who points out a possible solution. In his book *Answer to Job* (1952), the psychoanalyst Carl Jung comes to the conclusion that the true answer to Job only comes through the life and death of Jesus of Nazareth.

A God Slow to Anger

The short book of Jonah, in its own way, also explodes the limits of a too-narrow theology. The book was placed among the twelve minor prophets, but in fact it is a post-exilic fable using a historical figure to teach a lesson. The framework of the story is traditional: the prophet Jonah is sent by God to Nineveh, the vast pagan metropolis overflowing with wickedness, to proclaim God's judgment on its inhabitants. He refuses to go and flees from the Lord. We may well imagine that his refusal is motivated by fear, but the end of the book surprises us by disclosing the real reason for it. In fact, the prophet cannot stand the thought that the Lord may disregard his threats and forgive the wicked if they repent of their crimes:

> Jonah took it very, very badly, and got angry. He prayed to the Lord and said, "Is this not just what I said when I was living in my land? That is why I was so anxious to flee to Tarshish. I knew you were a gracious and compassionate God, slow to anger and overflowing with amiability and faithfulness, who relents from causing disaster." (Jonah 4:1–2)

The book of Jonah criticizes a certain Jewish superiority complex, that of people who are proud to serve "the Lord God of the heavens, who made the sea and the dry land" (1:9), while refusing to draw all the conclusions from this universal character of their deity. If God is the God of all, and if God is merciful, then will not God suffer to see human beings neglect their true happiness, and rejoice to see them return to him? That is what the conclusion of the book explains by means of the parable of the bush (4:6–8): if the prophet is so upset at the death of a small plant, does not God have the right to feel bad when human beings are lost, whoever they may be?

The book of Jonah helps us to understand a further difficulty that follows from the notion of impersonal anger used to explain historical events. In the final centuries of the pre-Christian era, another human and biblical theme begins to take on greater importance and interferes with our topic, perhaps under the influence of Greek thought, namely the notion of God as a just Judge who does not show partiality but treats everyone according to their deserts. In earlier days, the image of God as Judge was understood primarily as the one who restored justice to the world by taking the side of the weak and lowly against their oppressors:

> Judge me, O God,
> and take my side
> against a godless nation;

deliver me from deceitful and perverse people.
(Ps 43:1)

In a world where the powerful can act as they please, with no curbs on their behavior, God's impartiality meant, in fact, showing special attention to the poor. With the passage of time, however, the accent is placed instead on the judgment exercised by a detached referee, sitting above the fray, who gives to each person what he or she deserves. In the book of Sirach, a sage writing shortly before the Common Era, God's impartiality is still combined with the traditional preference for the humble:

> For he is a god of justice, who knows no favorites.
> Though not unduly partial toward the weak,
> yet he hears the cry of the oppressed.
> He is not deaf to the wail of the orphan,
> nor to the widow when she pours out her complaint.
> (Sir 35:12–14 NAB)

And the celebrated vision in chapter 7 of the book of Daniel likewise remains a transitional portrait. God is portrayed as an old man, the "Ancient of Days," frightening to look at, who is surrounded by a fire that consumes the powers of oppression (Dan 7:9–11). But he is also the eschatological Judge who sits on his throne, consults the books, and pronounces a judgment against some and for others (vv. 9, 10b, 22).

More and more, with the passage of time, it is the neutrality and objectivity of the judge that is brought to the fore; that is the new face of justice. A classical expression of this outlook is found in the well-known scene of the last judgment described in the Gospel according to Matthew (Matt 25:31–46): the sheep on the right, welcomed into the kingdom, and the goats on the left, sent away to "everlasting fire"; all the Judge does is to separate the two groups and pronounce the judgment.

It should be emphasized here that, for Jesus, this "separate but equal" status of the good and the wicked is far from being the true meaning of the story. As he often does, Jesus begins with a common event or a popular belief which he then modifies in the light of the gospel. Here, the point of the story lies in the affirmation that the ultimate fate of each person is determined, here and now, by welcoming (or not) the person in need, which in fact means welcoming (or not) the Messiah himself. But the framework of the story, doubtlessly reflecting the way people commonly imagined divine judgment, is eloquent testimony to the evolution of our topic: the wrath which previously stood for God's NO to evil has been transformed into an impersonal judgment, the paradoxical expression of divine justice. Paradoxical, because previously justice referred to the act by which God saved the poor and the oppressed by "rendering justice" to them—and the elimination of the oppressors was primarily a means to this—whereas now the accent is placed more and more on the condemnation of the wicked.

The conclusion of the book of Jonah helps us to see clearly, by contrast, what is most deficient in this new vision of things. The prophet is extremely irritated when the small plant that shaded him from the sun is destroyed, and God interprets this irritation as an expression of his pity (Jonah 4:9–10). In the same way, behind God's anger we sense that there lies hidden an enormous compassion for his wayward creation. In this sense, the book helps us understand that the sentence of condemnation, if it must indeed be pronounced, cannot leave God unscathed. It would cause God to suffer; one could almost say that it would represent a failure for him, in the same way that an educator trying desperately to help someone escape from an addiction feels she has failed when her attempts are unsuccessful, even though she may realize that she cannot make choices for the other person. In other words, in God, love and justice on the one hand, and anger on the other, can never be placed on the same level, as these images of an impartial judge might lead us to assume.

That is precisely what the expression "slow to anger," mentioned by Jonah, attempts to convey. The expression is part of a short creed or confession of faith that we find several times in the Hebrew Bible. It first appears in the book of Exodus, when Moses goes up to Sinai a second time to encounter the Lord. At that time, God reveals to him the divine identity:

The Lord came down in the cloud, and stood with him there, and he called upon the name of the Lord. And the Lord passed before him and proclaimed, "YHWH! YHWH! a compassionate and gracious God, slow to anger and overflowing with amiability and faithfulness, keeping his amiability for a thousand generations, bearing guilt, rebellion and sin, but not declaring the guilty innocent, visiting the transgression of the father upon the son and the son's son, to the third and fourth generation. (Exod 34:5–7; cf. Num 14:18; Joel 2:13; Jonah 4:2; Pss 86:15; 103:8; 145:8; Neh 9:17)

The first word used to describe God is *raḥum*, the adjective related to *raḥamim*, "the bowels," a word close to *reḥem*, the womb. It describes a deep attachment, literally a "gut feeling," like that of a mother for her baby, and is often translated "merciful" or "tender." Is it not striking that the God of the Bible, who some persist in seeing as a warrior or an angry judge, is described first of all by a "maternal" expression?

The second term of the first pair of adjectives is *ḥannun*, derived from *ḥēn*, "grace." This word describes the activity of a superior who descends to an inferior to bequeath a gift; it thus underlines the undeserved quality of divine love, motivated solely by who God is rather than by the character of God's partner. Following this there is another pair of words, *ḥesed* and *'emet*, which will often be used in the Scriptures to describe the God who wishes to make a covenant with human beings. The word *ḥesed*, usually translated by "steadfast love" or "kindness," is in fact a word that does not refer first of all to a characteristic or quality inherent in a person but rather to their way of acting, and specifically to their readiness to do what is necessary to establish and maintain a relationship, and to the acts accomplished to that end. The words used today to indicate this readiness would be "friendliness" or "amiability." The God of the Bible, far from being a deity immured in his splendid isolation, goes out searching for others in order to share their lives, to establish fellowship with them. And this word is paired with *'emet*, "truth" or "faithfulness." In the Bible, truth is not above all an intellectual quality, but evokes the fact that something or someone is really what it claims to be and therefore does not change; one can count on it. Here then, the God of the Bible is described as someone who seeks a relationship with his creatures, and the relationships God establishes are authentic, trustworthy, and lasting.

Between these two pairs of words, which are all in fact synonyms for love, we find the term "anger." But it is modified by an adjective that relativizes and even negates it: God is "slow to anger" (literally, God has a long nose!). In other words, although the notion of anger cannot simply be excluded from God, it is not a reflection of the divine identity. In himself God is always YES, but God is obliged as it were by the state of the world to say NO to certain things. As we have already seen, a God of love cannot say YES to anything that destroys life; God can never countenance evil. This NO, however, is not spontaneous; it is a kind of violence done to God by the absurdity of evil. In the face of sin, love turns into anger. In a word, in this ancient creed the NO is not eliminated, but it is clearly affirmed that it is in no way equivalent to the YES.

This same truth is expressed differently at the end of the passage. We are told that divine faithfulness and forgiveness last for "a thousand generations," whereas God pursues evil for "three or four generations." In other words, although evil continues to wreak havoc on others during the life of the evildoer, given that at most three or four generations can coexist at the same time, God's kindness is without end ("a thousand generations" means "forever"). The text should not be anachronistically understood as referring to personal moral guilt—at a later time it will be clearly stated that each individual is responsible for his or her own wrongdoing (cf. Ezek 18)—but rather to the consequences of evil, which do not merely affect the wrongdoer but spill over into the lives of other people as well as to the environment. This game of numbers, a thousand versus three or four, is a rudimentary but easily comprehensible way to affirm that, in God, love and anger are far from being equivalent. And this truth shows once again the main difficulty with viewing God as an impartial judge or referee who renders a verdict for or against the accused person with identical detachment. This rationalization of anger, by which it is transformed into a kind of impersonal law, obviously has the advantage of shifting the accent from God's reaction to the behavior of the evildoer who digs his or her own grave, so to speak. At the same time, by leaving us stranded in a universe where good and evil are in some sense equivalent, it disfigures the face of the One who has created a world where everything is "very good," and who desires the fullness of life for creation.

INTERMEZZO

LET US PAUSE FOR a moment to recapitulate our discoveries, before attempting to understand how the life and the message of Jesus the Messiah transform the theology of God's wrath.

1. The portrait of an angry god, a merciless judge, remains for many an obstacle to understanding the authentic message of the Bible. It leads either to a complete refusal of the faith or to a split between the God of the Old Testament and the God of Jesus Christ, an unfortunate and untenable division which the Christian church has combated from the very beginning.

2. Only a global and progressive reading of the Bible can avoid these pitfalls. The biblical message has to be understood in its integrity, as a narrative possessing a logic and a direction. This narrative is essentially the story of a good God, the Creator of a world that is "very good" (Gen 1:31), who wants life in fullness for his creatures and who attempts tirelessly to bring them out of the dead ends in which they get lost. All the individual passages find their true meaning within this overarching framework.

3. God's wrath or anger is not a fact but an interpretation of events. In order to gain a minimal understanding of the world of the divine, human beings are obliged to employ images taken from life on this earth. This procedure, although inevitable, involves a danger, that of projecting our own limits uncritically onto the divine. For this reason, a close and

critical reading is indispensable, one that attempts to comprehend what the text taken in itself and in its context means.

4. In ancient times, the sacred was seen as a power which comes from elsewhere and which has its own logic, often unsettling for human beings and sometimes involving negative consequences. It was experienced as an ambiguous energy.

5. In the oldest layers of the Bible, the God of Israel, like the deities of neighboring lands, sometimes appears as a warrior-god or as a storm-god. In archaic civilizations, upheavals of nature are a privileged location to discover the presence and activity of the gods. By their character both beneficial and destructive, such manifestations depict well the ambiguity of the supernatural world, its enigmatic quality.

6. In Israel, a tension appears very early between these impersonal manifestations of the sacred and the personal character of its God. Using the vocabulary of anger is an attempt to reduce this tension by interpreting the negative aspect of divine interventions. Although this procedure does not solve the problem fully, it already indicates a certain incompatibility between the world as it is and the world as its Creator wishes it to be.

7. On a human level anger, although it is rooted in the psychological makeup of human beings and therefore a universal phenomenon, takes on a great variety of expressions and meanings in different civilizations. In ancient Israel, it was the prerogative of rulers or the powerful, used as a way of affirming their authority. In this way it played a social role by contributing to maintaining the order of society. Within families or clans, the expression of anger generally had no serious consequences, whereas it could be fatal when directed against enemies.

8. Psychologically, human anger is the global—bodily, emotional, and mental—expression of the word NO! It is essential for human beings in the formation of their identity, since it sets limits to separate what is acceptable to them from what is not.

In itself, anger is neither good nor bad, but must be evaluated by answering the questions "What makes me angry?" and "How can this anger be used constructively?" Rather than being denied, it has to be integrated into the personality. In our day, particularly in Northern countries, people often have an unhealthy attitude towards anger, the other side of a permissive society. When considered shameful and therefore repressed, anger often has deleterious consequences. Moreover, this attitude explains in part the inability of so many of our contemporaries to understand the significance of divine anger.

9. Shorn of its anthropomorphic and mythological trappings, divine anger is the NO! of the God of life towards all that destroys life—in other words, evil in all its shapes and forms. A God who is good and who wishes to communicate this goodness to his creatures cannot tolerate anything that contradicts this project. The language of anger expresses the fact that evil is unacceptable and, in the final analysis, must disappear from the universe as its Creator intended it to be.

10. The prophets of Israel express this anger, in the name of God, towards a nation that is unfaithful and ailing because of this. Anger is thus the reverse side of God's indefectible attachment to his people; it bears witness to divine faithfulness in spite of the missteps of human beings.

11. In the prophetic books we find two different dimensions of God's wrath: an impersonal or outward dimension (Amos, Isaiah, etc.) according to which the wrongs of the nation automatically call down misfortunes upon it; and an inward or personal dimension (Hosea, Jeremiah, etc.) whereby the prophet experiences in the depths of his own being God's reaction to his partner's unfaithfulness. This second dimension reveals by analogy an inner struggle in God: anger turns into suffering and then leads to a deeper love.

12. The inward side of divine wrath remains relatively undeveloped in the Hebrew Scriptures. The outward side, however,

flourishes as a key to explain the ongoing progress of salvation history, notably in what is called the Deuteronomic history. In this narrative, Israel's unfaithfulness calls forth God's wrath, expressed by the calamities which fall upon the nation, and this leads to repentance and an act of deliverance by God, until the cycle begins all over again.

13. This theology of anger is not, however, shared by all. Biblical books like Qoheleth and especially Job, as well as certain Psalms, call into question a straightforwardly ethical vision of the world, where evil is always penalized and good rewarded. They witness to the fact that a solution to the problem of evil and the suffering of the innocent cannot come from within this world. The book of Jonah demonstrates the limits of this theology from another point of view, a more interior one: God cannot be resigned to the loss of his creatures, "for he does not afflict willingly nor grieve the children of Adam" (Lam 3:33). In himself God is only YES; the NO comes from the resistances of his partner and represents a kind of violence imposed upon him.

14. Even within the Deuteronomic theology, the image of an angry god tends to fade as a result of a progressive rationalization. Although "the wrath" still originates in a God who cannot tolerate evil, it is understood more and more as an objective reality, detached from God and functioning practically on its own. In the extreme case, it becomes a quality inherent in evil itself, by which sinners create their own misfortune by their acts; in essence they destroy themselves.

15. At the end of the pre-Christian era, another biblical theme begins to occupy the ground once filled by anger, that of judgment. The act of judgment at one time described God's intervention to save the needy from their oppressors, but now it becomes focused on another aspect, already present in the past (cf. Ezek 34:17, 20; 1 Kgs 3:16-28), but less central then—that of separating good from evil and giving to each person what he or she deserves. God the Judge is

seen more and more as an impartial referee standing above the fray, treating the wicked in exactly the same way as the good. This evolution, which expresses in its own way an extreme rationalization of anger, obviously has the advantage of eliminating the irrational and emotional dimensions from the portrait of God, but the cost is high: God's wrath, transformed into the judgment of sinners, tends henceforth to be subsumed under his justice. God is no longer "slow to anger"; wrath, disguised under another name, henceforth becomes part of the divine identity.

CHAPTER V

A Destabilizing Force

AT THIS POINT WE need to deepen our reflections on our topic in the light of the "Good News of the Messiah" (1 Thess 3:2; Rom 15:19, etc.). What happens to God's wrath after the life, death, and resurrection of Jesus the Christ? To find an answer to this question, the obvious place to begin is with the writings that make up what we call the New Testament. By examining them, we should be able to discover what changes took place after the coming of the Messiah. This enterprise, however, is not as easy as it may seem. The authors of the first Christian writings were Jews; they thought in the categories bequeathed to them by the religious history of their people. It took time for the yeast of the gospel to penetrate the dough of their traditions. It was only gradually that the disciples of Jesus grasped all the consequences of his appearance on the scene of history. In itself, this appearance marked an unprecedented break with the past—in Jewish terms, the transition from the previous age to a new age, from this world to the world to come. If there was continuity between the two, it was only at the cost of a still more radical discontinuity.

The first disciples of Jesus were well aware of this discontinuity, since it had been made evident to them by the death of their Master and the apparent shipwreck of all their hopes ("we were hoping that he was the one who was going to redeem Israel," say the discouraged disciples on the road to Emmaus [Luke 24:21]).

But they quickly discovered that Jesus' death was not the end of the story: restored to life, he incarnated for them even more clearly than before God's promise to his people. To express this promise that now had reached its fulfillment, the only language that the disciples had at their disposal was what they found in their Scriptures, our Old Testament. The first Christian theology was thus formulated largely out of biblical and Jewish notions and categories. And yet, by pouring the new wine of the gospel into the wineskins of the past, it was inevitable that at a given moment they would burst (cf. Mark 2:22). At the same time, faith in the risen Christ recombined the scattered fragments into a new synthesis: "And beginning with Moses and all the prophets, he explained to them what applied to him in all the Scriptures" (Luke 24:27).

This process of breaking things apart and putting them back together again—in a word, of transfiguration—was not a matter of a single day, or a year. In one sense, the need to "take prisoner every thought into obedience to Christ" (2 Cor 10:5) is a permanent dimension of any reflection on the Christian faith. For some elements of the gospel message, the central ones, the transfiguration occurred more quickly; for others, those on the periphery, the process required more time. The notion of divine anger, since it was not an essential component of God's identity but rather an indirect consequence of his activity, did not benefit from the work of reinterpretation as rapidly as other aspects of the faith. We should therefore not be surprised to discover, in the pages of the New Testament, a significantly great diversity in the way this notion is understood and expressed. At the same time, we will notice particular accents in the way divine wrath is understood with respect to the previous tradition, as a result of the Passover of Christ.

Saved from the Wrath

In the previous chapters, we distinguished between two dimensions of God's anger, an impersonal or outward dimension and a personal or inward one. In this chapter, we shall investigate impersonal anger. A preliminary, and quite striking, difference in the New Testament with respect to the Old is the virtual absence of what we have called explanatory anger—in other words, anger seen as a key to understanding the history of salvation by means of the interplay between the unfaithfulness of God's people and God's own faithfulness. For his part, Jesus refuses to explain misfortune as a divine punishment for sin, at least in the personal lives of women and men:

> At that time some people informed him about the Galileans whose blood Pilate mingled with their sacrifices. He replied, "Do you think that those Galileans were sinners more than all the others, because that happened to them? No, I tell you, but you will all perish in the same way if you do not change your ways! Or those eighteen people on whom the tower in Siloam fell and killed, do you think that they were any guiltier than all the inhabitants of Jerusalem? No, I tell you, but you will likewise perish if you do not change your ways!" (Luke 13:1–5)

Similarly, in John's Gospel:

> Passing by, Jesus saw a man blind from birth. And his disciples asked him, "Rabbi, who sinned, that man or his parents, because he was born blind?" Jesus replied, "Neither he nor his parents. It was so that the works of God might be manifested in him." (John 9:1–3)

Impersonal anger in the New Testament follows instead in the steps of prophets such as Amos and Isaiah, broadened by the so-called apocalyptic outlook current in the final centuries before the Common Era. Here anger is focused on the future, and is not linked to one specific event but is an element accompanying the end of the present world. The New Testament book considered by many to be the oldest, Paul's first letter to the Thessalonians, already shows the particular bent this topic receives in the light of Christ Jesus. Paul describes Jesus as the Son of God, risen from the dead, whom we await from heaven and "who rescues us from the wrath to come" (1 Thess 1:10; cf. Rom 5:9). And he explains: "God did not destine us for wrath but to obtain salvation through our Lord Jesus Christ" (1 Thess 5:9). We see here the continuation of a usage that we already observed before the coming of Christ, namely the *depersonalization* of anger. In the New Testament writings, nowhere do we find God depicted as someone who gets angry. Often, as here, "the wrath" is simply mentioned as a reality possessing its own consistency. Rather than being considered as a feeling or an attitude belonging to God, it tends to become in essence a technical term to describe the consequences of evil. It remains *God's* anger, to be sure, in the sense that these consequences only appear in the light of the revelation of the divine identity, culminating in the life and work of Jesus. But it is stripped of all irrational personal elements and functions in a way similar to the bad karma of the Eastern religions, as a kind of law inherent in the functioning of the universe, a process that follows the logic of cause and effect, with the significant difference that, for the Bible, this universe was created by God and becomes comprehensible only in relationship to him.

A second characteristic of the evocation of anger in the New Testament is its subordination to the good news of life. It is never presented for itself alone, but always as the other side of salvation. Christ *saves* us from the wrath to come, says St. Paul; we are not destined for wrath but for *salvation*. It would not be an exaggeration to say that the notion of wrath is important for the apostle only to the extent that, if one is saved, one must obviously be saved *from* something. In this sense, the word "anger" can easily be replaced by other terms such as "death" (Rom 6:16; cf. Rom 4:15 and 7:10) or "ruin, destruction" (cf. 2 Cor 2:15; 4:3; 2 Thess 2:10). And in his letter to the Galatians, Saint Paul speaks of Christ "who rescues us from the present evil age" (Gal 1:4). As the consequence of the refusal of a free gift that calls for a free response, anger is a kind of shadow cast by the manifestation of love.

In his letter to the Romans, Paul develops this topic at length (Rom 1:18–32). Here we see the same tendencies at work. The main theme of this letter is the gospel as the revelation of God's justice or righteousness—in other words, the divine plan of salvation for the created universe and God's faithfulness to this plan, despite the manifold obstacles erected by the misuse of human freedom. After having said that through the gospel "God's justice is revealed" (Rom 1:17), immediately afterwards the apostle continues: "God's wrath is revealed," precisely not by means of the gospel, but "from heaven against all human godlessness and injustice" (1:18). In other words, by manifesting the culmination of his loving designs through the coming of his Son, God causes the other side of the coin to appear even more clearly, the reason for which this divine intervention was necessary—the self-destructive behavior of human beings.

This is reinforced by the way in which this wrath works itself out. In this context, three times Paul uses the verb "to hand over": "God handed them over to impurity . . . to dishonorable passions . . . to their undiscerning minds" (1:24, 26, 28). The apostle is undoubtedly alluding to the fact that, in the Old Testament, in his anger God sometimes hands over evildoers to their enemies instead of protecting them (cf. Judg 2:14; 1 Kgs 8:46; 2 Chr 6:36; 36:16–17; Pss 78:58–61; 106:40–41; Ezek 21:36). In this way, Saint Paul wants to show that God is not the one who causes the consequences of inauthentic human behavior to emerge; it is rather the behavior itself that causes suffering and leads to perdition. Previously, God had not revealed to human beings the full extent of their distance from him. Out of concern for them, he shielded them from the full realization of their condition, fearing that it might lead them to despair. Now, before the cross of Christ, the true situation of humanity is laid bare.

Looking at the same process from another angle, we can discern in it the great respect which God has for human freedom. God never forces people's hearts, but continues to hope that human beings, after following their perverse logic to the end, will return to authentic life in communion with their Creator. For this reason, a few verses later, Paul criticizes those who think they can save themselves by responding to evil with an attitude of judgment and condemnation of their fellows. When you judge others, he writes, "do you imagine that you will escape God's judgment, or are you disparaging the riches of his kindness, forbearance and patience, unaware that this kindness should lead you to repentance?" (Rom

2:3–4). Hasty condemnation risks short-circuiting a process of transformation (cf. 1 Cor 4:5), and destroys the solidarity which is the fundamental law of creation; God, for his part, acts differently. At the same time, however, it cannot be denied that those who continue to walk on the road of evil enter into an apparently inexorable cycle: they "accumulate for themselves a treasure of anger for the day of wrath" (Rom 2:5; cf. Jas 5:3; Eph 5:6; Col 3:6) or, as Saint John puts it, "God's wrath looms over them" (John 3:36). Anger here is, in the final analysis, the mechanism by which sin leads to spiritual death. At work throughout the ages, it is manifested, indirectly but definitively, by the coming of Christ: "Anyone who is not with me is against me, and anyone who does not gather with me scatters" (Luke 11:23).

The Day of Judgment

In the New Testament, the manifestation of God's wrath is associated with two other themes, forming an amalgam which does not always facilitate our understanding. The first of these themes is the *Day of the Lord*. The prophets of ancient Israel, having to deal with situations of injustice and faced with people unwilling to search for the Lord's will and put it into practice, looked for a new manifestation of God's power that would put things to right by eliminating evil and establishing justice. Little by little, this "Day" took on an eschatological quality—in other words, it was seen as marking the great turning-point of history, the end of the present state of affairs and the beginning of a new age. It thus had two different aspects: the collapse of the present world, or at least everything in it that contradicted God's intentions, and the establishing of "new heavens and a new earth, where justice dwells" (2 Pet 3:13). It is perhaps not surprising that, in the popular imagination, it was the negative side that prevailed, so that "the Day" became a synonym for devastation and anguish. In this sense, the texts sometimes speak of "the Day of wrath," *dies irae* (Zeph 1:15; Rom 2:5).

The other motif that interfered with that of anger was the notion of *judgment*. We have already looked briefly at the evolution of this topic in biblical thought. At first representing the coming of the Lord to establish his justice by liberating the poor and unfortunate from their oppressors, over the centuries its meaning shifted. This change was aided by the translation of the Hebrew word into Greek, which placed the accent not on the establishment of a just society but rather on the separation between the good and the wicked. The judge was no longer primarily the savior of the unfortunate, but rather the referee who "will repay each person according to their deeds" (Ps 62:12; Rom 2:6). At the same time, the faithful identified themselves less strongly with the victims of the violence of those holding power and became more aware of their own guilt: "Do not enter into judgment with your servant, for no one alive is in the right in your eyes" (Ps 143:2). As a result of this evolution, judgment became not something to be looked forward to with joy but an event to be feared. As with the Day of the Lord, the negative aspect predominated, so that "to judge" became in essence a synonym for "to condemn," a radical reversal of its original meaning. This evolution was certainly aided by the context in which the notion was employed. Far from being a simple description of divine activity, the reminder of judgment was almost always used as a warning to reawaken the slumbering consciences of believers.

The Gospels follow for the most part this vision bequeathed to them by the tradition, especially since, during Jesus' life on earth, the Day of the Lord and the judgment are still seen as future events. Jesus and his disciples thus take as their starting point the same understanding of these realities as their Jewish contemporaries.

In the Gospels, the Day of the Lord becomes what Luke calls "the day when the Son of man will be revealed" (Luke 17:22–37) and Matthew "the sign of [Christ's] coming (*parousia*) and the end of the age" (Matt 24:3). A comparison of the announcement of the end in the first three Gospels (Matt 24; Mark 13; Luke 17, 21) reveals a diversity of approaches, undoubtedly due to the fact that each Gospel writer adopted common elements according to his own concerns. They depict a preliminary period of dissension and hostility among humans, the destruction of Jerusalem and the temple, cosmic upheavals, the Savior's coming "with great power and glory" (Mark 13:26), threats and exhortations to perseverance, etc. The final composition appears to be a mixture, impossible to sort out, between the teachings of Jesus himself and expressions found in the apocalyptic literature in vogue at the time. It is clear at any rate that the final coming of Christ, for which the beleaguered disciples are longing, entails the disappearance of "this age," a world dominated by the forces of evil.

This section of Matthew's Gospel ends with the great scene of the last judgment (Matt 25:31–46). In some of Jesus' other sayings, the day of judgment (Matt 12:36) is described as a future event that will reveal the hidden truth of the present and, above all, the true meaning of people's attitude towards Jesus and his disciples. The fate of those who turn their back on him will be worse than that of the pagan cities Sodom and Gomorrah (Matt 10:15), or Tyre and Sidon (Luke 10:12–15; Matt 11:22–24). They will be condemned by the people of Nineveh and by the Queen of the South (Matt 12:41–42; Luke 11:31–32). In these sayings, the purpose of the judgment is to reveal the true state of affairs, and Jesus' reason for speaking in this way is not to pronounce a definitive condemnation, but to convince his hearers of the importance of the present moment and the choice that needs to be made. It is not surprising that this is exactly what we find in the final judgment scene in Matthew 25: the definitive fate of human beings is not reserved for an indeterminate future, but takes place here and now, in the attitude I show and the actions I perform towards "the least of these brothers and sisters of mine."

This shift of the accent from the future to the present is reinforced by the vision of judgment in John's Gospel. Although the fourth Gospel does not formally deny the notion of a future judgment (cf. John 5:29; 12:48; 1 John 4:17), it constantly affirms that the essential occurs in the present moment, in each person's relationship with Christ Jesus:

> The Father judges no one, but has given all judgment to the Son . . . . I tell you the truth: anyone who hears my word and believes in the One who sent me has eternal

life and does not come to judgment, but has crossed over
from death to life. (John 5:22, 24)

John's Gospel helps us understand even more clearly that
Jesus does not speak of a judgment in order to satisfy our curios-
ity concerning the world to come; he does so to emphasize the
importance of the choices to be made in the present day. By presenting things in this way, John follows a logic that is also found
in the parables of Jesus. These stories often end with an alternative
between life and death, depending upon whether one welcomes
the good news or refuses it. The consequences of a refusal, which
correspond to the theme of God's wrath, are expressed differently
according to the logic of each parable; it would be pointless to attempt to harmonize them all. The most common images are fire
and darkness.

A classic image of supernatural power, *fire* has a destructive
side which is appropriate to evoke the destiny of evil. During the
harvest, for example, the wheat will be gathered into the barn while
the chaff "will burn with fire that never goes out" (Matt 3:12); in
another story, the same is true for the weeds (Matt 13:40). This
inextinguishable fire is often related to *gehenna* (Mark 9:44–48;
Luke 12:5, etc.), the traditional place of reprobation which origi-
nally had a precise geographical location, the ravine of the sons
of Hinnom (Jos 15:8) or the Valley of Hinnom (*gē-hinnōm*, Neh
11:30) southwest of Jerusalem. In a distant past, it was apparently
the place where the god Moloch was worshiped, a cult involving
child sacrifice. Later on, it became the dump where the rubbish of
Jerusalem was burnt, night and day. It thus became an unambigu-
ous symbol of the place where the dregs of the earth end up; it
describes graphically the ultimate destiny of everything that resists
God's loving designs.

The other principal symbol used in the Gospel parables to
evoke the consequences of evil is the *outer darkness*. Those who are
thrown out of the place of joy and celebration typically react with
"weeping and gnashing of teeth" (Matt 8:12; 22:13; 25:30; cf. 24:51;
Luke 13:28), which is not an expression of physical suffering, but

rather one of regret and anger at being excluded from the feast.[1] The parable of the invited guests who do not come to the banquet, as told by Luke (14:15–24), shows the true meaning of this image of exclusion. Here those invited are the ones who exclude themselves, preferring to remain attached to their private concerns rather than to accept the generous and perhaps unexpected invitation of the rich man. In his anger, the host merely draws the ultimate conclusions from their unwillingness to take part in his banquet: "I assure you, none of those I invited will taste my dinner" (v. 24).

Finally, some parables express the same thing using other images. The fig tree with no fruit will be cut down (Luke 13:9); what the fishermen catch by mistake will be thrown out on the seashore (Matt 13:48); the desiccated branches on the vine will be burned (John 15:6). As is often the case, Saint John helps us to understand best the deeper meaning of these images. The branches are dry and without grapes because they are already no longer part of the vine. In other words, the exclusion does not come from the side of God; what is already dead, and therefore useless, is simply eliminated.

The Storm Is Coming

This cluster of traditional themes taken up in the Gospels—Day of the Lord, judgment, fire, destruction—is likewise found in the other New Testament books. Since in these books the authors describe the existence of believers in the wake of the death and resurrection of Jesus, we need to ask ourselves what consequences this change of perspective has for our topic. This question has to be given a nuanced answer. Certain books of the New Testament, the ones on the margins, for instance the Second Letter of Peter and the Letter of Jude, apparently maintain a traditional outlook

---

1. It should be noted that we find these stereotyped images of "unquenchable fire" and "weeping and gnashing of teeth" above all in Matthew's Gospel. Mark, usually considered the oldest Gospel, does not employ them, nor does John, and Luke uses them more sparingly. This fact by itself alone should dissuade us from emphasizing too strongly their importance for Jesus, still less from treating them as a literal description of "hell."

which is essentially unchanged. The punishment of evildoers—here referring mainly to false Christian teachers—is described in terms where the gospel seems to play no role at all, except that the condemnation is more radical than ever, because after the coming of the Messiah God has spoken his final word and there is nothing else left to hope for (2 Pet 2:20–22; cf. Heb 10:16–31). Still, even in these extreme cases it is clear that the goal of the exhortation is to convince believers to stay on the right path, remaining faithful to Christ come what may.

Elsewhere, too, the same traditional themes are taken up by the New Testament writers. The Day is imminent (Heb 10:25), although it is not yet here (2 Thess 2); it will come like a thief in the night, when no one is expecting it (1 Thess 5:3). At the judgment (Jas 5:12; Heb 9:27), when the living and the dead appear before God (1 Pet 4:5), each person will be judged according to their works (1 Pet 1:17; Rom 2:6–11; cf. Col 3:25), and the judgment will be without mercy for those who have shown no mercy (Jas 2:13). In certain cases, however, Christ replaces God as the main actor. The authors speak of "the Day of our Lord Jesus Christ" (1 Cor 1:8; Phil 1:6) or the "judgment seat of Christ" (2 Cor 5:10). Sometimes, despite the change of name, the circumstances are practically the same. In the Second Letter to the Thessalonians, the Lord (Christ) comes "in a blazing fire, to take vengeance on those who do not know God and who do not obey the Gospel of our Lord Jesus Christ; they will incur the penalty of eternal perdition far from the face of God" (2 Thess 1:8–9). Writing to the Corinthians, Paul emphasizes for his part the revelatory dimension of the judgment, similar to the words of Jesus in the Gospels: "He will shed light on what is hidden in darkness and reveal the intentions of people's hearts, and then each person will receive from God the approval that they deserve" (1 Cor 4:5).

We can conclude from these passages that the destruction of evil and the elimination of all that does not correspond to God's loving designs, as well as the personal responsibility of each person, are an integral part of the biblical message both before and after the coming of the Messiah. Must we be satisfied with that conclusion? Does the way God is portrayed here not still betray a split personality, with mercy on one side and condemnation on the other? Fortunately, certain New Testament passages take things further by helping us to understand how these truths can coexist with a God who is "slow to anger" and even has no explicit intention to destroy. Already, the parable of the two houses (Matt 7:24–27) sets us on the right road. Two men each build a house, perhaps identical except for a single detail: one is constructed on rock and the other on sand. Then the storm begins: "the rain fell and the torrents came and the winds blew" (vv. 25, 27). One of the houses stands firm in the tempest; the other collapses. The difference here does not come from the side of God—love on the one hand, anger on the other—but one and the same event leads instead to opposite results.

Saint Paul adapts this image to the situation of his readers by applying it to the judgment:

> Each person must take care about the way they build. No one can lay any other foundation than the one which has been laid down, namely Jesus Christ. If someone builds on the foundation in gold, silver, precious stones, wood, grass, or straw, the work of each person will become evident. For the Day will make it manifest, because it will be revealed by fire; the fire will put to the test what sort of work each person has done. If a person's work of building survives, that person will receive their reward. If it is consumed by the fire, they will suffer the loss. That person will be saved themselves, but as it were by passing through the fire. (1 Cor 3:10–15)

The very same fire reveals the quality of each person's work. The Letter to the Hebrews expresses the same thing in another way, quoting some words of the prophet Haggai:

> The one whose voice shook the earth in the past has now made this promise: One more time I will shake, not only the earth, but heaven too. The words "one more time" signify the removal of what has been shaken, namely created realities, so that what is unshaken will remain. Since we have received an unshakable kingdom, let us hold on

to this generous gift. . . . For our God is a consuming fire.
(Heb 12:26–29)

In all these texts, the final coming of God is seen as a destabilizing force that overturns all the ramparts erected by humans to
defend their identity and to justify their choices. After the storm
passes, they find themselves face-to-face with God in all their vulnerability, and this lack of obstacles enables them to receive a share
in the divine life. What could look like anger, seen from without,
is revealed in fact to be a "jealous" love that does not tolerate
any halfway measures but which wants to take possession of its
partners in order to transform them completely, like iron which
becomes incandescent in a furnace.

A Harsh and Dreadful Love

As for many other biblical topics, the final stage in the evolution
of impersonal anger is found in the writings of Saint John. The
beloved disciple succeeds in uniting the single-mindedness of
God's attitude and activity—God is not of two minds (cf. Jas 1:8;
4:8), but can do nothing but love—with the personal responsibility
of each man and woman. In addition, John emphasizes strongly
that the essential of what we call judgment does not occur in an
indeterminate future but rather in the present moment, through
the encounter with Jesus the Christ.

In his conversation with the Jewish leader Nicodemus, Jesus
explains all this by employing an image of extreme simplicity, the
image of light. He begins by saying:

> For this is how God loved the world: he gave his only
> Son, so that all who believe in him do not perish, but
> have eternal life. For God did not send his Son into the
> world to judge the world, but so that the world might be
> saved through him.[2] (John 3:16–17)

---

2. For reasons both of syntax and content, the expression "God so loved the
world" should be understood in this way, and not be taken to mean "God loved
the world so much," as it is in most translations.

God has only one intention: since God is love (1 John 4:8, 16), God can desire nothing but to share this love with creation—in other words, to "save" it. It is extraordinary that, for Saint John, here even the desire to judge, to separate good from evil, still less to condemn evil, does not enter explicitly into God's outlook. Nonetheless a separation does occur, one could almost say automatically:

> Whoever believes in him is not judged; whoever does not believe has already been judged, for that person is not a believer in the name of God's only Son. (John 3:18)

And by means of the image of light, Jesus explains how and why this takes place:

> This is the judgment: the light has come into the world, and people preferred the darkness to the light; this was because their deeds were evil. For whoever does evil hates the light and does not come into the light, so that what they do does not come to light. But whoever does the truth comes into the light, so that it might be manifest that their deeds have been done in God. (John 3:19–21)

At a later moment in the fourth Gospel, Jesus repeats this way of looking at things:

> I have come into the world as light, so that whoever believes in me does not remain in the darkness. If someone hears my words and does not keep them, I do not judge that person; for I did not come to judge the world but to save the world. Whoever rejects me and does not receive my words has their judge: the words I have spoken will be their judge on the last day. (John 12:46–48)

In other words, in his Son, God excludes no one from his love, and that is why Jesus can say "I will not cast out anyone who comes to me" (John 6:37). Nonetheless, in the face of this unconditional love, the inexplicable mystery is that some people do turn away: "You do not want to come to me to have eternal life" (John 5:40). In the final analysis, such individuals act in this way because, in their self-sufficiency, they do not think they need Jesus:

> Jesus said, "I have come into this world for a judgment, that those who do not see may see and that those who see may become blind." The Pharisees who were with him heard these words and said to him, "So we are blind, too, are we?" Jesus said to them, "If you were blind you would not be guilty, but since you say 'We see,' your sin remains." (John 9:39–41)

The clearest example of this self-exclusion is the case of Judas, one of the twelve men closest to Jesus. During the last supper, it is at the very moment when Jesus gives him a tangible sign of his love by expressing his communion with him that the process is set in motion:

> Jesus gave the morsel of food that he had dipped into the wine to Judas Iscariot, the son of Simon. When he gave it to him, at that moment Satan entered into Judas. . . . He took the morsel and left at once; it was night. (John 13:26–27, 30)

It is pointless to speculate about the ultimate fate of Judas. What is obvious is that he is mentioned in the Gospels in order to give concrete form to the horrifying possibility that a person can close him- or herself to the light. Human beings, bequeathed with the inestimable gift of freedom by their Creator in order to love—for love is the freest act possible—can use this freedom in a contradictory fashion to express a refusal, turning it against its true end. Here it becomes clear that the NO by which we defined the essence of anger is not in the final analysis a reality in God. God, as revealed by his only Son, is only YES (cf. 2 Cor 1:19). Saint John helps us to understand that the NO that we think we see in God is in fact the mirror image of our own NO—in other words, of our attempt to set ourselves up in an illusory autonomy and so cut ourselves off from our Origin. Judas is not cast into the outer darkness; he goes there freely.

In these Johannine texts, all that the traditional biblical topics of anger and judgment were meant to express is absorbed, as it were, into the image of the light, for "God is light, and there is no darkness at all in him" (1 John 1:5). But we should not imagine that this is a facile solution which removes from the Christian faith its seriousness and its radical character. God's love is not an undemanding, watered-down benevolence, but a life-force that never says "enough" (cf. Prov 30:16). Dorothy Day, the founder of the Catholic Worker movement in the United States, which sets up communities of sharing with the poor and excluded and that undertakes radical acts of nonviolence against injustice, was deeply touched by some words of the *starets* Zosima in Fyodor Dostoyevsky's novel *The Brothers Karamazov*: "Love in action is a harsh and dreadful thing compared to love in dreams." This is because such a love places human beings before the truth of their being, removing all their rationalizations and self-justifications. As that beautiful and enigmatic book of the Bible, the Song of Songs, expressed it several centuries before Jesus:

> Love is as fierce as death,
> passion is as harsh as Sheol,
> its flames are flames of fire,
> blazing flames.
> Floods of water cannot extinguish love
> and rivers will not submerge it.
> (Song 8:6–7)

Changing Our Outlook

Let us now attempt to sum up our discoveries concerning the evolution of impersonal anger in the light of the gospel of Jesus Christ.

In the wake of the great prophets of Israel and after the widening of perspectives in the centuries before the Common Era, divine wrath became seen as the flip-side of the definitive revelation of God during the great turning-point of history, the transition from this age to the age to come. At that moment, everything that is an obstacle to Love will be swept away, "so that God can be all in all" (1 Cor 15:28). This definitive revelation of God in his Day also involves a judgment—in other words, a critical moment that manifests the true identity of each woman and man and makes possible a choice for or against life.

The gospel adds an important complement to this vision: the turning point of history has already become a reality in the life, death, and resurrection of the Son of God, even if all the consequences of this change of regime are not yet apparent on the surface of human history. The way divine anger is understood, therefore, depends upon the attitude of every human being towards Jesus the Christ. For those who do not yet know him or who do not want to accept him, "God's wrath looms over them" (John 3:36); it is an inescapable part of their universe, hovering on the horizon. To put it another way, a threat of destruction hangs over all their accomplishments, even the most brilliant. Outside of Christ, human beings inevitably experience the devastating consequences of their waywardness, which lead only to death. Moreover, they are inclined to interpret the course of history as the antipathy of God (or the gods) to them, sometimes represented as a cruel and inexorable fate, or even a "tale told by an idiot, full of sound and fury, signifying nothing," as Shakespeare's Macbeth puts it. To the extent that their existence expresses a NO to the loving will of God, this NO is projected into the heavens, so to speak; it forms part of the face of God that they see. God's love for and trust in his creatures is experienced as a threat. They react like the third servant in the parable of the talents or mines, who said to his master: "I was afraid of you, because you are an exacting man, who exacts what he did not invest and who harvests what he did not sow" (Luke 19:21). We should note that this way of understanding the master's identity—incorrectly, as shown by the attitude of the other two servants—becomes the rule that will be applied to him: "I am going to judge you on the basis of your own speech, wicked servant" (Luke 19:22). In his Sermon on the Mount, Jesus even turns this into a general rule: "You will be judged by the judgment with which you judge, and be measured by the measure with which you measure" (Matt 7:2; cf. Jas 2:13). Outside of the full revelation of the mystery of God to which we have access through Christ, the world remains ultimately enigmatic, absurd, or even hostile; the opposition between good and evil appears to be fundamental and irreconcilable.

On the other hand, "there is no condemnation at all for those who are in Christ Jesus" (Rom 8:1). When a man or woman adheres to Christ through faith and baptism and begins to live a new life "according to the Spirit," they experience a reversal of perspective. They receive a new way of looking at God and the world, although it may take time for this new perspective to enter fully into their existence and to transform it. But the great turning point has already occurred; with Christ they have passed over from death to life (cf. John 5:24; 1 John 3:14). In this new way of looking, they no longer see any contradiction in God. It is as if they have taken off a pair of glasses that gave them double vision. They now realize that God is love and love alone, and what they understood previously as anger was simply the encounter between that love and all that interferes with its full realization, like a torrent that washes away everything that stands in its path. The devastating aspect of God's coming is shown to be, in reality, the self-destruction of evil. Or, to change the image, the same fire that purifies by devouring evil communicates a beneficent light and warmth (cf. Mal 4:1–2). In God, all is simple; the contradiction comes from our side, as a result of our inner divisions.

The access to this new vision of things is not the fruit of human reasoning. According to Saint Paul, it takes place "in Christ Jesus"; it is the fruit of his mission to our earth. Consequently we need to ask ourselves: how does this metamorphosis occur? How does Jesus make possible this transmutation of divine wrath into mercy unlimited? These questions lead us now to consider the other dimension of anger, its personal or inward side, and the transformation this undergoes in the light of the gospel.

CHAPTER VI

The Man of Sorrows

IN OUR INVESTIGATION OF prophetic anger in the Hebrew Scriptures, we identified two different dimensions. Although the prophets of Israel invoked divine wrath most often to warn the nation of the consequences of behavior contrary to God's justice, some of them experienced this anger in their own existence. A Hosea or a Jeremiah interiorized the message they received to such an extent that it left its mark on their own inner life. Thus their personal reactions, beyond their words, became a language through which God could communicate with humanity. In this respect, one can speak of a movement of incarnation, by means of which the message does not fall down directly from heaven but slowly takes shape from within the human condition.

The followers of Jesus of Nazareth believe that this movement of incarnation finds its culmination in him. To confess him as the Son of God, or the Word of God, entails holding the conviction that the Creator of the universe is fully revealed in a human life. This means that the entire existence of Jesus is revelatory, not just his words or certain spectacular acts he accomplished. In this chapter, then, we will attempt to examine how our topic is expressed and transformed in the personal existence of Jesus, notably in his inner life.

Preliminary Difficulties

Exploring Jesus' inner life is not an easy task, and there are several reasons for this. First of all, even for people close to us, what they are actually thinking or feeling is not always evident. We can only try to guess what is taking place within them from their words or actions, by placing ourselves hypothetically in a similar situation. And the more distant we are from someone in space, time, or culture, the more difficult it is to understand that person's inner dispositions. Who has not written an email that was misinterpreted by its recipient because the words on the screen, absent the tone of voice and any facial expressions, remained ambiguous and so were read in a way far different from what the sender intended?

In the case of Jesus, not only does a considerable temporal and cultural distance separate us from him, but his unique identity keeps us from simply attributing to him the same motives which may have prompted us to act in a similar situation. Moreover, all we have from him are sayings and stories which, before being written down, were passed on from one person to another. We must accept the fact that we have no direct access to the historical Jesus; our understanding of him is inevitably mediated through others. To this is added the additional difficulty that the vocabulary used by the Gospel writers to describe his states of mind is far from being unequivocal. Terms for feelings and emotions differ enormously from one language to another and from one civilization to another, not to mention the variations among the four Gospels themselves. All this is a reason for extreme prudence. Nonetheless, while taking these difficulties into account, and basing ourselves on what we have discovered in the preceding chapters, let us attempt to ascertain how Jesus experienced and dealt with anger.

Jesus' no

We can begin by recalling our definition of anger as the global expression of the simple word NO. Rather than starting from the descriptions of Jesus' inner states in the Gospels, therefore, we will first of all try to answer the question: what are the realities to which Jesus expresses a firm NO by his attitude and behavior? In this context, the verb *epitimaō*, "to rebuke, admonish, threaten," can offer us some useful indications.

Jesus opposes his NO first and foremost to the forces of evil. In the world of his time, these destructive powers or beings were omnipresent, and seen as the cause of illnesses and accidents. Thus Jesus rebukes and casts out an unclean spirit (Mark 1:25; Luke 4:35), the fever that attacks Simon's mother-in-law (Luke 4:39), and demons (Luke 4:41). When the disciples are endangered by a storm on the Sea of Galilee, Jesus rebukes the wind and the waves (Mark 4:39). These forces of nature evoke the primeval chaos, and here Jesus is implicitly identified with the Creator who establishes the harmony that makes a peaceful existence possible. Finally, after his temptations in the wilderness, Jesus sharply dismisses Satan, the personification of these malevolent powers (Matt 4:10). In all this, Jesus embodies the wrath of God that rejects everything which destroys the life and peace of the world.

In relationships between people, Jesus views anger as an unacceptable means of settling differences, considering it a form of homicide (Matt 5:22). And yet, this does not keep him from expressing annoyance at certain groups of people and opposing his NO to them, above all those who abuse their spiritual authority. This means above all "the scribes and Pharisees," the religious elite of the nation, and what Jesus criticizes in them is the dissonance between their inner life and their public role: they speak well, but do not act accordingly (cf. Matt 15:1–9; 23:1–36; Luke 11:37–54). They are *hypokritai*, a term usually transliterated as "hypocrites" but whose original meaning is "stage actors." Such a gap between what lies in the depths of one's being, which the Bible calls the heart, and what is shown to others makes people impermeable to the message of Jesus. It reduces faith to external rituals rather than letting it be what it is—a transformation of the entire person under the influence of the Spirit of God. In addition, when leaders who have not been transformed inwardly claim to teach the truth to others, their words, emptied of any real content, lose all credibility and present a false image of God and his desires for us. Such teaching, rather than intriguing and attracting the hearers, causes them to leave the right path and go astray (cf. John 10:5). Jesus is merciless when speaking of this:

> Brood of vipers! How can you say good things when you yourselves are evil? The mouth speaks from what overflows from the heart. (Matt 12:34)

The disciples themselves are not spared the criticisms of their Teacher. Jesus tells them that those who claim to belong to him without doing what God wishes will one day hear these dreadful words: "I have never known you; get away from me, you wrongdoers!" (Matt 7:23). When Peter attempts to give Jesus advice on how he should accomplish his mission, he hears this vehement response: "Get behind me, Satan!" (Mark 8:33; Matt 16:23). And the only time in the four Gospels that the verb *aganakteō*, "to be indignant, angry," is used to describe the attitude of Jesus is when his disciples refuse to let children come to him (Mark 10:14). On another occasion, he states:

> If anyone causes one of these little ones who believe to stumble and fall, it would be better for that person to have a huge millstone tied around their neck and to be cast into the sea. (Mark 9:42)

This is followed by harsh words about the importance of not acting in a way that causes oneself or others to lose faith: "If your hand or foot causes you to stumble and fall, cut it off . . . if your eye causes you to fall, pluck it out" (Mark 9:43–47). And Luke, who, of all the Gospel writers, is the one who most emphasizes Jesus' kindheartedness, nonetheless tells this story:

> They entered a Samaritan village to prepare for him. And the people did not welcome them, because they were heading for Jerusalem. Seeing this, the disciples James and John said, "Lord, do you want us to call down fire from heaven to burn them up?" But he turned to them and rebuked them. (Luke 9:52–55)

Finally, Jesus expresses his indignation at those who set themselves up as judges of others (Matt 7:1–7) and those who ask for a sign before trusting him (Luke 11:29–32; Matt 12:38–39; cf. John 4:48). All these examples express an "anger" that does not aim to destroy its object or lessen the humanity of the person concerned, but rather wants to establish clear boundaries that must not be crossed in order to remain in the space where God's promise can bear fruit.

A Provocative Act

The clearest example of Jesus' anger is undoubtedly the scene where he casts out the buyers and sellers from the temple of Jerusalem. Recounted in all four Gospels, this event can scarcely have been invented after the fact and attributed to Jesus by the disciples, since such a violent act is a far cry from the traditional portrait of a Jesus who is "gentle and humble of heart." The first three Gospels place it at the end of Jesus' public life, whereas John situates it at the beginning of his Gospel. The former date seems more plausible; one can easily see it as a last-ditch attempt to incite a conversion in people after the apparent failure of words.

If many people today find this act shocking and uncharacteristic of Jesus, that is probably because they are unfamiliar with the biblical context. In fact, it easily takes its place in the long line of prophetic acts with a provocative intent. Like Jeremiah acquiring an earthenware jug and shattering it in front of the crowd (Jer 19), like Ezekiel shaving his head and beard with a sword and dividing the hair (Ezek 5), like Hosea marrying an unfaithful woman (Hos 2), Jesus hopes that his exaggerated behavior will lead the spectators to become aware of the great discrepancy between the will of God ("a house of prayer for all nations") and the daily life of the nation ("a den of robbers"). The purpose of the act was not to harm human beings, nor seriously to disrupt the ongoing life of the temple—in fact it must have been a fairly limited action, otherwise the authorities would have reacted swiftly, and even the improvised whip mentioned by John was undoubtedly in order to get the animals moving. Its intention was rather symbolic, to get people to start thinking and to represent clearly the condition of Israel in God's eyes. In addition, like the prophets before him, Jesus put his own life on the line by exposing himself in this way.

In Mark's Gospel, the incident takes place during the last days of Jesus in Jerusalem and is sandwiched in the middle of the story of a fig-tree that bears no fruit and is cursed by Jesus (Mark 11:12–21). The two symbolic acts have the same meaning: they dramatize the fact that the final hour has struck for Israel. In rejecting Jesus the official nation, represented by its elites and centered on the institution of the temple with its worship, has clearly demonstrated that it is unable to discern and to follow the will of God. Jesus's anger acts out in advance the fate of those who cling to their inauthentic behavior and refuse to open themselves to God, who comes to them in the person of his beloved Son (cf. Mark 12:1–12). It thus offers a final possibility for them to change their ways, while at the same time serving as a portent that this appeal will not be heard.

From Anger to Sorrow

In our reflections on prophetic anger in Hosea and Jeremiah, we noted an inner transformation in them. The prophet's solidarity with his wayward compatriots transforms his vexation at their unfaithfulness into a deep sorrow. The anger is directed inward and turns into sadness, the expression of a love which has been rejected. A similar evolution can be found in Jesus, and provides an important key to understanding the mystery of redemption.

There is, however, a significant difference between Jesus and his predecessors. In their case we find a dramatic progression: first, anger with destructive intent is expressed, and then a reversal occurs when the prophet realizes that by hurting the loved one he hurts himself even more. In Jesus, things do not follow this pattern. No fundamental shift of outlook can be discerned in him. Simplifying a bit, we can say that anger and sorrow coexist in him as part of a more complex whole, manifesting themselves by turns according to the requirements of the situation. In Jesus, solidarity predominates, expressing itself as irritation or frustration when his hearers do not understand what is at stake, in the implicit hope of awakening in them an awareness of their obstinacy. If, in the end, sadness and suffering gain the upper hand, that is because the time is over when a NO clearly expressed can hope to change anything. In Jesus, anger remains from beginning to end an expression of love.

A tiny but precious indication of this relationship is found in a passage at the beginning of Mark's Gospel, which contains as well a problem of textual criticism:

> A man with a skin disease came to him, falling on his knees and begging him, saying "If you wish, you can make me clean." Jesus *took pity on him* and, reaching out his hand, touched him and said to him, "I do wish it; be clean." And immediately the skin disease left him, and he was cleansed. Jesus gave him strict orders and sent him away at once. (Mark 1:40–43, emphasis added)

In some manuscripts, instead of the verb translated "to take pity" (*splangchnistheis*), we find the verb *orgistheis*, "to get angry." Following the rule of the *lectio difficilior*, by which the more incongruous alternative is seen as the original one, some bible scholars consider the latter word to be more original. It is obviously much easier to imagine that a scribe would have changed anger into compassion than vice versa. Still, the best manuscripts have *splangchnistheis*, and so most commentators prefer that version.

Whatever the solution to the textual problem may be, in the light of our reflections, an explanation of Jesus' anger in this situation would not be hard to find. His irritation is not directed against the sick person himself, but against the powers of evil that have preyed on him to keep him from living a full life. The theme of irritation appears again later in the story (v. 43, translated here as "gave him strict orders" but containing a nuance of annoyance). In addition, the verb *splangchnizomai* comes from *splangchna*, "the intestines, bowels." It is most probably a Semitism, since the equivalent word in Hebrew is *raḥamim*, which means both the bowels and compassion. We should recall that in the passages from Hosea and Jeremiah describing the movement from anger to love, an inner agitation is mentioned, a turmoil that resembles the pains of childbirth (cf. Hos 11:8; Jer 31:20). Would it not then be possible to see, beneath the surface of Mark's story, an implicit link between anger and compassion? Confronted with someone who is suffering and outcast, Jesus is appalled, understanding better than anyone how much this sickness contradicts God's desires for his creatures. In the depths of his being, this aversion to evil joins up with his love for the man and his solidarity with him, leading to a healing. The essential takes place within Jesus himself. His compassion is literally a suffering-with.

A similar indication can be found in the reaction of Jesus one Sabbath day in the synagogue, when the onlookers remain silent in order not to consent to the healing of a man whose hand is paralyzed:

> Looking around at them with anger, deeply grieved at
> the hardening of their hearts, he said to the man . . .
> (Mark 3:5)

In the face of hearts closed to life, Jesus' attitude cannot be reduced to a single human emotion. His attitude has a negative side, which both witnesses to and struggles against evil. In doing so, it takes up the best of the theology of divine wrath in ancient Israel. No more than his Abba, Jesus cannot consort in any way with the refusal of life. At the same time, as a result of his solidarity with human beings far from God, Jesus cannot place himself in the position of someone who judges from without. His attitude thus also includes a deep sadness, a heartfelt suffering at his deluded brothers and sisters. Without the NO of anger, human responsibility and the meaning of human acts would not be taken seriously. But without com-passion, suffering-with, Jesus would not be the Son of a loving God. In Jesus, therefore, anger and sorrow are two sides of the same coin.

The Other Side of Anger

Let us now examine more closely this other side of Jesus' attitude towards human beings trapped in the snares of evil. A first stage on the continuum that goes from anger to compassion is the *frustration* of Jesus when confronted with a lack of trust in God and in him. He sighs deeply when the Pharisees ask for a sign in order to believe in him (Mark 8:12); they are "an evil and adulterous generation" (Matt 12:39; 16:4), a code word used in the Hebrew Scriptures to describe Israel when it forgets its calling (cf. Ps 95:10–11). Saint John emphasizes Jesus' astonishment, a milder form of annoyance, at the hesitations of the Jewish leader Nicodemus: "You are a teacher of Israel and you are unfamiliar with these things?" (John 3:10). Jesus is likewise astonished at the lack of faith of the inhabitants of Nazareth, and he can do nothing for them (Mark 6:5–6), since trust in him is essential in order to enter into the new life he wants to offer.

Speaking to the crowds, Jesus uses a striking image to describe his annoyance at those who cannot understand, or do not wish to:

> To whom will I compare the people of this generation? Who are they like? They are like children sitting in the town square and shouting to one another: "We played the flute for you and you did not dance; we sang a dirge and you did not weep." (Luke 7:31–32; Matt 11:16–17)

Jesus even shows his impatience at his disciples when they do not grasp the significance of his words (Mark 8:14–21; Matt 16:5–12) and are unable to continue his ministry (Mark 9:18–19); they too are a "faithless generation." To the apostle Peter he says these poignant words reflecting both exasperation and sadness: "Man of little faith, why did you doubt?" (Matt 14:31). A similar disappointment is evident in these words to Philip, reported by Saint John: "I have been with you for such a long time and you do not know me, Philip?" (John 14:9).

At certain moments, this frustration reaches the breaking point and turns into profound sorrow, the sorrow of someone whose deepest intentions are not understood and who feels betrayed by his closest friends, the pain of a disappointed lover. An emblematic expression of this pain in the biblical texts is the simple Greek interjection *ouai*, a translation of the Hebrew *'oy* or *hoy*, in English "woe" or "alas." Particularly common in the preaching of the prophets, it is often considered a threat, or even a curse. But the roots of this Hebrew expression are rather to be found in rites of mourning; it should be seen first and foremost as a lament.

It is in this spirit that Jesus employs the expression fairly often in the Synoptic Gospels. A confirmation of the fact that it is a lament, and not a threat, comes from Luke's version of the Beatitudes (Luke 6:20–26). The word *makarios*, sometimes translated as "blessed," is not in fact in the language of the Bible a blessing—in other words, the act of calling down good things upon someone—but rather a celebration of the fact that the individual or group in question is well-placed to benefit from what God offers. In everyday English we would say, "How lucky you are!" while realizing that luck as such is not part of the biblical worldview. As a result, the four "woes" that follow are not curses, but the affirmation that the people they describe are on the wrong road. It is as if Jesus were saying, "How unfortunate for you . . ." Although a nuance of correction may well be contained in the expression, along the lines of "if you do not change, things will not go well for you," its main significance is that of regret, of sorrow at seeing someone lose their way.

Thus Jesus expresses his heartfelt sorrow at the cities of Galilee because of their inability to receive the offer of salvation that is being extended to them through his coming: "Alas for you, Chorazin! Alas for you, Bethsaida!" (Matt 11:20–24; Luke 10:13–15), for you are missing the most important opportunity of your entire existence. This lamentation of Jesus at the hardness of heart of his fellows comes to a climax in the words spoken over the Holy City, Jerusalem, which functions as a symbol for the entire nation. In Matthew's Gospel, these words come towards the end, just after the woes against "the scribes and the Pharisees," the spiritual elite of the nation, and before the announcement of the destruction of the temple and the end of a whole world. They thus express the "judgment" of Jesus concerning his rebellious people, where lucidity combines with a note of hope and where the Judge experiences in himself the suffering that the guilty are not (yet) able to feel:

> Jerusalem, Jerusalem, you kill the prophets and stone those sent to you! How many times have I wished to gather your children together as a hen gathers her chicks under her wings, but you did not want it. Now see, your home is going to be left deserted. For I tell you, you will not see me again until you say: Blessed is the one who comes in the name of the Lord. (Matt 23:37–39)

Saint Luke places the same passage earlier in his Gospel (Luke 13:34–35), but he takes the same subject up again later, in an even more poignant fashion:

> When he came near to the City and saw it, he burst into tears over it, saying, "If you, even you, had only known, on this day, the things that lead to peace! But now they have been hidden from your eyes!" (Luke 19:41–42)

The tears of Jesus are an eloquent symbol of the transformation of anger into sorrow. This NO to an inauthentic life, when it is not heard by those for whom it is destined, returns to the one who pronounced it and is just as painful for him because, in his beloved Son, the Creator has completely espoused the existence of the creatures.

My Soul Is Sorrowful to the Point of Death

It may be helpful to restate here the thesis of this chapter, in the awareness that it may strike many as peculiar, or even incoherent. Jesus' response to evil and to those who make common cause with it, the equivalent of the biblical theme of divine wrath, is a complex and dynamic attitude which includes both irritation and sorrow. It begins as a kind of expression of displeasure in human terms, with the intention of inducing those to whom it is addressed to change their ways or, if this is not possible, at least of dramatizing their failure. But as things move forward, faced with the growing incomprehension and refusal of his hearers, Jesus internalizes his irritation, in which case it becomes a blend of sadness and suffering. It is as if Jesus, seeing the inability of human beings to respond to the love offered them by a love in return, takes this inability into himself and suffers its consequences to the end.

Since this activity takes place for the most part within Jesus, it is not easy to discern; his outward sufferings are only a dramatic transposition of it on the level of historical events. The moment it becomes most clearly visible is undoubtedly the visit made by Jesus and his disciples to the Mount of Olives, just before his passion and death. There Jesus, at grips with the reality of evil, experiences an intense inner combat (*agōnia*, Luke 22:44), which Mark and Matthew attempt to describe using the verbs *ekthambeō* (Mark 14:33, "to be astonished, disturbed, alarmed, frightened"), *adēmoneō* (Mark 14:33; Matt 26:37, "to be upset, distressed, deeply troubled"), and *lupeō* (Matt 26:37, "to be sad, sorrowful, distressed; to grieve"). These expressions are obviously imprecise; the inner life of Jesus remains enigmatic for us, and even to a certain extent a closed book. Still, a close examination of this passage enables us to go beyond the superficial impression that Jesus was primarily at grips with the fear of the atrocious suffering that lay before him. Physical suffering can certainly be dreadful, and at times unbearable, but life offers us a host of examples of people who consent to suffer for their children, for their country, or for a cause. Unwillingness to suffer cannot explain, all by itself, the reaction of Jesus in Gethsemane.

We should notice that the description of Jesus' state of mind in the garden turns around two poles—first, an inner upheaval and, secondly, sadness. To describe this upheaval, Saint John, for his part, prefers to use the verb *tarassō*, "to shake, agitate" (John 12:27; 13:21). Confronting the reality of evil without the defenses we usually erect causes us to lose our usual points of reference and casts us into turmoil and confusion. In these pages, we have often described anger as the expression of a NO in the face of what is unacceptable. When this unacceptable reality is interiorized by someone who has not given an inner consent to it, since God can never say YES to evil, it causes the foundations of their being to totter. The NO of anger, by a kind of boomerang effect, wreaks havoc upon the innocent person who absorbs it in total vulnerability. It is like swallowing poison: it is not for nothing that Jesus uses the image of the (bitter) cup he has to drink (cf. Ps 75:8), an eloquent symbol of the consequences of human evil, in biblical terms of anger. If Jesus feels an intense aversion for the contents of this cup, that is not because he is afraid to suffer, but because it is the polar opposite of divine goodness. Yet he consents to drink it, with a trust almost totally obscured by the darkness of evil, that in God this act will somehow bear fruit: "Will I not drink the cup that the Father has given me?" (John 18:11).

Just as strong as the distress that Jesus feels is the great sadness that fills him. Transforming into sorrow, motivated by love, the anger directed against an outward evil, Jesus recapitulates his experience in these words in Gethsemane: "My soul is sorrowful to the point of death" (Mark 14:34; Matt 26:38). We can hear here a distant echo of the words of the prophet Jeremiah in a similar situation:

> If you do not listen,
> I will weep in secret at your pride;
> my eyes will weep, shed bitter tears:
> the Lord's flock has been taken captive. . . .
> Let my eyes shed tears,
> night and day, without ceasing,
> for a great blow has crushed the virgin daughter of my people;
> she has been afflicted with a terrible wound.
> (Jer 13:17; 14:17)

Images of grief and mourning are frequent in the book of Jeremiah, and Jesus' sadness is likewise an expression of grief. Grief is, in its essence, a participation in the death of a beloved individual. Those close to the deceased share his fate, in a certain sense, by their behavior. Mourning is thus the expression of a solidarity that in some cases can go to the point of identification. When Jesus says, "My soul is sorrowful to the point of death," is he not affirming that the death he is going to suffer is in reality that of human beings who have turned their backs to true life? Out of love Jesus shares in this death and makes it his own. But—and this was not true of Jeremiah and the other prophets—he remains the beloved Son, joined to his Abba by an unbreakable communion. For this reason, his death is not simply an ending but a new beginning, the dawn of new life.

What the experience of Jesus in Gethsemane attempts to show is expressed in the fourth Gospel by the story of Lazarus. When Jesus arrives at the tomb of his friend, who has been dead for four days, and sees the relatives and acquaintances of Lazarus in mourning, he "was deeply moved and shaken" (John 11:33). Since the word translated by "to be deeply moved" can also mean "to rebuke" and the other verb is *tarassō*, here we see once again the mixture of irritation at evil and inner turmoil that we have noted in Jesus on several occasions. Then, immediately afterwards, the other dimension appears: "Jesus wept" (John 11:35). The death of someone he loved reveals in Jesus the twofold emotion anger/sorrow. But here a further step is taken compared to the Mount of Olives. Sighing deeply once again, Jesus calls to the dead man and Lazarus comes out of the tomb. Saint John thus anticipates the fact that Jesus' combat against evil leads to a victory. Chapter 11 of his Gospel helps us understand that the resurrection, far from being a magic wand waved to resolve an impossible situation, is the culmination of Jesus' entire life, a struggle to the very end by which the energies of anger transform from within death into life.

Happy Those Who Mourn

In the previous chapter, we saw that God's wrath is presented in the New Testament as part of the great turning-point of history; it is the shadow-side of the new age promised by God and realized by the coming of the Messiah Jesus. Outside of Christ, it is thus a reality that is not yet complete; it is still on the horizon. It corresponds to the decomposition of a world built on sand, often described in the texts using images of a cosmic cataclysm (e.g., 2 Pet 3:10–12), the prelude to "new heavens and a new earth, where justice dwells" (2 Pet 3:13). These images are not meant to be taken literally. They refer primarily to the world fabricated by human beings forgetful of their Creator, as is most clearly shown in John's Gospel.

It is Christ "who rescues us from the wrath to come" (1 Thess 1:10). Those who follow him have already passed over from death to life. They have consequently realized that all God can do is love, and that what seemed to be utter destruction was in reality liberation from an inauthentic existence. Now, after our investigation of the inner journey of Jesus, we are better able to grasp how this passage from destructive anger to liberating mercy could occur. The essential movement is this: in the face of the obstinate refusal of human beings to listen to God's NO and to change their behavior, Jesus takes this NO fully into himself and suffers the consequences. In so doing, he transforms a form of negative energy, which had been turned outward, into sorrow and suffering fully consented to out of love.

It is this refusal by his human sisters and brothers, to whom he nonetheless remains faithful, together with his faithfulness as the beloved Son to the loving will of his Father, that leads Jesus to an atrocious death. But his outward sufferings, however terrible they may have been, do not give us the key to understanding his mission. The key is found in the will to assume, out of love, the consequences of human nonacceptance of the life offered by God. At this point, some luminous words of a young Italian woman of the fourteenth century, Catherine of Siena, come to our aid: "Nails were not strong enough to hold God-and-man [fastened on the Cross.] No, it was love that held him there."[1] By his life, Jesus thus offers us the best commentary on the third Beatitude in Matthew's Gospel: "Happy are those who mourn: they will be comforted" (Matt 5:5). By sharing the death of those who are far from God, in an unbreakable solidarity, Christ enables the energies of life to flood their existence. However outlandish it may appear at first sight, the tears of Jesus are in fact his anger, fully assumed and transfigured from within.

1. Noffke, *Letters*, 66.

We are now capable of grasping the grain of truth present in those appalling theories from the Reformation of the sixteenth century onwards, in theology but even more in popular preaching, that explained redemption as the consequence of God's wrath descending upon Christ, the innocent victim. For example, this anonymous text, possibly from the sixteenth century:

> It is written: *It is a terrible thing to fall into the hands of the almighty God.* And here sweet Jesus, because of us, spontaneously, lovingly handed himself over, allowing all the wrath, the rage and the punishment of God the Father, which we deserved, to fall upon him.

And here is Bossuet, a celebrated French bishop and preacher, a century later:

> And so, my brothers, [God] had to act against his Son with all his thunderbolts; and since he had placed our sins in him, he also had to place in him his just vengeance.[2]

These explanations are repulsive to us, and rightly so, in the first place because of the implicit image of God to which they bear witness—a sadistic divinity, determined to satisfy his wrath come what may, even if it has to be vented on an innocent being. They are even more wrongheaded because they imply a fatal dissociation within the Trinity, by which the hardheartedness of the Father is compensated for by the kindness of the Son. We encounter a similar split in certain forms of Catholic piety where Mary, the mother of Christ, was at times presented as a compassionate mother ready and willing to divert the wrath of her Son, by placing herself between us and his arm ready to strike. Those who imagine such things have apparently never realized that by exalting one of the actors to the skies, they dishonor the other and make him unrecognizable. Instead of presenting the faith as a mystery of communion, they transform it into a struggle between opposing parties.

---

2. These texts, and others, are in Sesboüé, *Jésus-Christ l'Unique médiateur*, 67–83.

There is nonetheless a core of truth in the affirmations we have just quoted, glimpsed confusedly and expressed in an extremely inept manner by the authors. Our reflections have showed us that, in his passion and death, Christ Jesus absorbs into himself divine wrath and in this way allows love to flow freely. But this anger does not come upon him from the outside, through the condemnation of a heartless judge who, in some inexplicable fashion, has taken the place of his loving Abba. On the contrary, as the beloved Son, Jesus shares the outlook of his Father completely and utterly ("the Father and I are one," John 10:30), expressing the very same NO to all that destroys life. However, since Jesus, in addition to being the Son of God, is simultaneously the Son of Man who lives in total solidarity with his brothers and sisters, he suffers with them and for them the consequences of their waywardness. In fact, he suffers more than any of them, for in him there are no defenses, no refusal; he is total openness and vulnerability. The NO to evil becomes fully interiorized in him.

In the Bible, anger is normally expressed in a situation where God stands before his recalcitrant people in a face-to-face relationship. But when the gap between the two poles has been done away with, in the one whom Catherine of Siena calls God-and-man, then anger takes on the shape of a "sorrow unto death" by which Jesus consents to giving his life to the very end. The essential difference is thus not between the Father and the Son, but between a God who is situated at a certain distance from the human condition and a God who, in his only Son, fully espouses our condition. When God is no longer seen as a being exterior to us—and this becomes fully possible only in Christ—the divine energies that took the form of anger are revealed as a fire within humanity that consumes evil and makes us transparent to life. As Brother Roger, the founder of Taizé, used to say, all God can do is love, but this love is manifested unambiguously only on the cross of Christ. By his Passover through death to life, Jesus "took away death's power and caused life and immortality to shine forth" (2 Tim 1:10). In him there can be no more fear, "because fear implies punishment, and the one who fears has not been made perfect in love" (1 John 4:18).

One of the foundational texts of Western civilization is *The Divine Comedy*, the work of the Florentine poet Dante Alighieri (1265–1321). That long poem takes up and explicates the traditional vision of life after death in medieval Christianity, divided into three "places": hell, which represents the sufferings of those who close themselves off totally from God's love; purgatory, a time of purification before entering fully into the divine intimacy; and paradise or heaven, the expression of a total communion between God and human beings. This framework was never current in the Eastern church nor in the Protestant world, and such a three-story construction need not of course be taken literally. But the poet's journey does give us a useful base for summing up, in a single sentence, our investigation of divine wrath in the New Testament. *In Christ, hell is revealed as purgatory, the anteroom of paradise.*[3] For "there is no longer any condemnation for those who are in Christ Jesus" (Rom 8:1).

3. The same intuition from another point of view is found in Lewis, *The Great Divorce*, 68–69.

Coda

The Wrath of the Lamb

An investigation of the last book of the Bible, known as the book of Revelation or the Apocalypse of Saint John, will put our reflections on the evolution of biblical anger to a severe test. A cursory examination of this book could easily give the impression that we have taken a step backward compared to what we have already seen in the New Testament. So many images of conflict and destruction, and very little mention of mercy and solidarity. At times we seem to find ourselves in the middle of a holy war, where threats and violence have the upper hand. It is not surprising that many Christians prefer to put this book aside, uncertain how to deal with it. Is there any chance, in spite of everything, that it can help us in our attempt to discover the authentic meaning of the topic of divine wrath in the Bible?

How to Read the Apocalypse

Most of the difficulties that arise in reading the book of Revelation are due to a misunderstanding of its purpose and its style. It belongs to a very special literary genre, as different from the other New Testament books as a Jules Verne novel differs from a history of France in the nineteenth century or a copy of the daily newspaper *Le Figaro* from those same years. The title of the book already sets us on the right road: *Apocalypsis Iēsou Christou.* The Greek word *apokalypsis* comes from the verb *apo-kalyptō* (Latin *re-velare*), meaning literally to uncover or to unveil (from Greek *kalyptra,* Latin *velum,* "veil"). The visions that John had on the Isle of Patmos, far from being a literal description of present or future events, disclose a deeper reality, hidden beneath the veil of our habitual perceptions.

The words *Iēsou Christou,* which modify the first term, should be understood as both a subjective and objective genitive. In other words, Jesus Christ is both the revealer and the revealed. As "the faithful witness" (Rev 1:5; 3:14), the one who recapitulates God's plan from the origin of the universe to its end (cf. Eph 1:9–10), he unveils his own mystery to believers. The visions of John are thus a revelation of the true meaning of history, normally hidden from our eyes and culminating in the mystery of Christ.

Where does this veil, which keeps us from seeing the universe and human beings as they truly are, come from? It originates, in a word, in our self-centered vision of reality. By considering everything starting from ourselves, both individually and collectively, by projecting on others and on events what we desire or fear rather than seeing them objectively for what they are, we leave behind what is real and root ourselves in the world of illusion, called *Maya* by the Hindus. This is not, of course, an illusion in the sense that these realities do not exist, but because they are fatally distorted by the way we look at them, as a function of our self.

The visions of the Apocalypse, then, lift the veil of illusion and enable us to see what is really going on. This reality, however, is not directly translatable into human words or concepts. It must come to us indirectly, through images, in a language that can be called poetical or mythical. More specifically, the images that populate the book of Revelation are almost all taken from the Hebrew Scriptures, our Old Testament. That is what may give us the impression, in reading this book, that we are returning to a previous and outdated stage of religious consciousness. In fact—and this is the secret of the Apocalypse and the challenge of its interpretation—the old images and concepts are transfigured from within, by the light of Christ shining on them. In this sense, too, the last book of the Bible recapitulates the entire course of revelation: if it is read independently of Christ, it inevitably appears anachronistic, but if it is understood in the light of the gospel, it reveals the astonishing unity of the biblical message. "When someone turns towards the Lord, the veil is taken away" (2 Cor 3:16).

The Self-Destruction of Evil

In the first place, the visions of the seer of Patmos recapitulate and bring to a head what we have called external anger in the Bible. This is what gives the book its apparently violent character. In order to understand this theme, we shall look first at its climax and then work backwards.

Let us begin with an image that we have already briefly encountered in the story of Jesus at Gethsemane—the bitter cup. In the ancient world, the cup was often a symbol of destiny; it was not rare for the gods to hold a cup in their hands, perhaps to cast lots. In Israel, however, blind destiny did not exist. In the Bible, the universe created by God has an ethical quality (see chapter 4): by their behavior, human beings accumulate a treasure either of justice or of injustice, and the day will come when they experience the consequences of this. We thus find, in the Psalms, the cup of blessing on the one hand (cf. Ps 16:5; 23:5; 116:13), and the bitter cup on the other (cf. Ps 75:8).

The book of Revelation culminates in a great opposition between two cities. First there is Babylon, the city of iniquity that sums up all the resistance to God throughout history and that, in John's time, was symbolized by the Roman Empire. Later on, Babylon is replaced by its antithesis, the new Jerusalem that comes down from heaven, "the dwelling-place of God with human beings" (Rev 21:3). When Babylon is destroyed, we read: "Babylon the Great was called to mind before God, to give her the cup of the wine of his furious wrath" (16:19; cf. 14:10). The city of iniquity finally falls under the weight of its own wrongdoing. For if this cup is given to her by God, upon closer analysis we realize that its content comes in fact from Babylon herself. The city is described as a great prostitute who "held in her hand a great cup full of abominations" (17:4). "She gave all the nations the wine of the frenzy (literally: fury) of her prostitution to drink" (18:3), and what she inflicted upon her victims is finally turned against her: "Pay her back with the same money that she has paid out, and give her the double of what she has done. In the cup where she mixed her potions, mix her the double" (18:6). The city of iniquity has prepared its own fate; the divine Judge is there simply to guarantee that the energy of evil does not destroy innocent victims but becomes in the final analysis a form of self-destruction.

We see this very same process in chapter 11. "The nations raged, but it was your anger that arrived . . . and the destruction of those who were destroying the earth" (11:18). But all that is only the necessary prelude to the creation of a renewed universe.

The cup of anger is linked to a similar image, the last of the septenaries or groups of seven that are found as a *leitmotiv* throughout the book:

> And I heard a loud voice from the Temple saying to the seven angels, "Go and pour out the seven bowls of God's fury on the earth." (16:1)

The word translated by "bowl" is not exactly a cup, but a shallow container used in worship to carry ashes, to drink or to offer the liquid offerings known as libations. The image thus describes a liturgical rite. But we would not be wrong to see these seven bowls as the extension of the same movement recapitulated in the cup given to Babylon: the manifestation of the ultimate consequences of human evil. The bowls, emptied by the angels upon the earth, cause torments that recall the plagues that came upon Egypt to liberate God's people from bondage (Exod 7–11). They have a twofold purpose: to contribute to the disappearance of a world set up in opposition to God; and to serve as a warning to those who are in collusion with that world, by causing them to realize that they are on a road leading only to ruin.

In fact, the seven bowls are the final act of a crescendo that runs through the entire book. In chapters 8 to 11 we encounter another septenary, seven trumpets blown by angels. Each time the trumpet sounds, something falls from heaven to the earth and causes great damage. The first four trumpets are concerned with the material universe, and they are followed by three "woes" (Greek *ouai*, see previous chapter) that affect humankind. The first of the woes (9:1–12) presents locusts that resemble scorpions, who torment by their stings—a frightening depiction of what today we call addiction. The following woe (9:13–21) is similar: horses that harm by their mouths and their tails. We should notice that the woes themselves do not come from God—the first one arises from the abyss and the second comes from beyond the river. God simply allows them to devastate humanity.

If we go back to the septenary preceding this one, we discover the primary cause of all this suffering. Chapters 4 to 6 of the book of Revelation paint a striking picture. We first see a mysterious being composed of light, seated on a heavenly throne and acclaimed as Creator of the universe (ch. 4). In his right hand he holds a scroll sealed with seven seals, in all probability his project for creation. But no one is able to read it, until another being comes forward: a lamb standing, looking as if it were slaughtered. The lamb takes the book and begins to open the seals (ch. 5). The vision thus shows us that it is Christ alone, dead and risen, who can reveal the mystery of the created universe and of human history in all its breadth and depth.

The first four seals (6:1–8) form a unity. They describe four horsemen, riding different-colored horses. The first one, on a white horse, comes to conquer, a verb which generally has a positive meaning in this book. Although this interpretation is not shared by all, should we not see here an evocation of humanity, made in the image of God and destined to participate in God's sovereignty over creation? The situation quickly deteriorates, however. The second horse, fiery red, stands for war, and the third, black, for famine. All this leads to the fourth horse and rider, pale green, which is Death and which slaughters a fourth of the earth. We have here summed up very dramatically, the fate of humanity without God: opposition among human beings followed by a lack of sharing among them and, finally, a broken relationship with the earth, leading ultimately and inexorably to death.

What we have called external anger is the divine response to this situation. It is a persuasive way of saying that this kind of behavior contradicts the will of God for his creation. It can thus serve as a warning, but at the same time it attests to the fact that, in a universe which is the handiwork of a good God, evil has a self-destructive character. If the warning is not heard, the destruction escalates: a fourth (6:8), a third (8:7–12), and finally the whole (ch. 16). If one stage is apparently missing, that of a half, this is ostensibly because another septenary, the thunders (10:3–4), was not revealed, perhaps to shorten the time it takes for the old world to disappear (cf. Matt 24:22). For—and this is the final message of the Bible concerning external anger—in the final analysis, the manifestation of the consequences of evil does not succeed in slowing down its progress:

> And the rest of the people, those who were not killed in these plagues, did not repent of the works of their hands, turning away from the worship of idols of gold, silver, brass, stone and wood, idols that cannot see or hear or walk. They did not repent of their murders or their magic practices, nor of their sexual immorality or their thievery. (9:20–21; cf. 16:11)

Anyone who considers this statement an exaggeration has only to look at the recent history of our planet. The twentieth century saw two horrific world wars, with a total of over seventy million victims. It is not clear, in spite of this, that something fundamental has changed in international relations that would portend an era of peace for the world. The same could be said about our destruction of the natural environment, which proceeds apace in spite of the climactic and geographical disturbances that are already making themselves felt. To bring about a world according to the wishes of its Creator, the self-destruction of evil—external anger—is manifestly not enough. Another starting-point must be found.

A Paradoxical Victory

To speak of the coming of God's reign on the earth, the Apocalypse often employs the noun "victory" and the verb "to conquer." This is the vocabulary of war, and martial images do play an important role in this book. But if we examine the use of this language carefully, we will discover once again that it has been subverted from within to describe a completely different reality.

In chapter 5, for example, when the seer is disheartened because no one is able to read the scroll in God's hand, he hears these words: "Weep no more! See, the Lion of the tribe of Judah has conquered, the Root of David" (5:5). We are then primed to see the Messiah of Israel appearing in the guise of a victorious warrior, but instead the passage continues:

> Then I saw,
> in the midst of the throne and the four living creatures
> and in the midst of the elders
> a lamb standing, who appeared to have been slaughtered.
> (5:6)

The inhabitants of heaven acclaim him by singing a new song:

> You are worthy to take the scroll and to break the seals,
> because you were slaughtered
> and have purchased for God, by your blood,
> people of every tribe, language, people and nation
> and you have made them a kingdom and priests for our God
> and they will reign on earth. (5:9–10)

The victory of the Messiah is thus, paradoxically, the gift he makes of himself out of love. The lion, king of beasts, is manifested on earth as a lamb, the most vulnerable of animals and the sacrificial victim par excellence. The blood by which the victory occurs is not the blood of God's enemies shed on the battlefield, but the blood of Jesus himself, which flowed from his heart pierced on the cross (cf. John 19:34). This blood becomes a vast river which "flowed from the vat to the height of horses' bridles for a distance of 1,600 stadia (over 180 miles)" (Rev 14:20). In it, those who follow the lamb are able to wash their robes and make them white (cf. 7:14), forming "a great multitude that no one could count, from every nation and tribe and people and tongue" (7:9).

At this point, the inconsistency of those who insist on interpreting the Apocalypse as a literal description of events that will take place in the future becomes manifest. These people say, in effect: "Certainly, during his life on earth Jesus was gentle and humble of heart. He did not respond to evil with evil, or to violence with violence. But, at the end, towards those who have not accepted him, he will act differently. He will show his true colors by waging a war of extermination against them. The time of mercy is over; henceforth vengeance will gain the upper hand. As the saying goes, no more Mister Nice Guy." Such an attitude, barely exaggerated here, would mean that the Son of God was not truly revealed in the Gospels. He was wearing a mask that he would ultimately remove.

If we maintain, on the contrary, that the Jesus of the Gospels does show us the true face of God, and if the visions of the seer of Patmos are authentic in their turn, then we are forced to interpret them in the light of the entire gospel message. The victory of Christ consisted in his faithful love, a love that brought him to an ignominious death. It was a paradoxical war, where the winner achieved victory by losing in human terms. In the same way, his followers are victorious by continuing Jesus' works to the very end (2:26), by their perseverance and their faithfulness in the midst of trials (13:10; cf. 14:12). "They follow the lamb wherever he goes" (14:4). "They did not love their lives to the point of fearing death" (12:11). It is this apparent defeat that brings the old world to an end and prepares the coming of the kingdom of God.

The Great Day of Wrath

Let us return now to the vision of the seven seals, which provides the basic framework for understanding God's plan. After the opening of the first four seals, which depict the inevitable downward course of a world without God, John shows us the other side of the coin. God has not forgotten his creation, and will now set out to bring it back to himself, although in a totally unexpected fashion. The fifth seal describes "the souls of those who had been slaughtered for the Word of God and the witness that they gave" (6:9). We can see in them all the innocent victims of human injustice across the centuries (cf. 18:24; Matt 23:35). They cry out to God and call for justice. The verb *ekdikeō*, sometimes translated by "to take revenge," means here that they are seeking to be vindicated; they want to have it made clear that their cause has been heard and that their suffering was not in vain. They are told that they must be patient for a little while longer (6:11), but that their appeal has been taken into account. In this book "the prayer of the saints," into which their undeserved suffering has been integrated, is in fact the strongest motive-force of human history (cf. 5:8; 8:3–5), more efficacious than all the superficially impressive maneuvers of the violent.

The sixth seal provides the key that enables us to understand just why the suffering of the innocent is so powerful and effective. Deciphered correctly, it represents the culmination of the biblical teaching on divine wrath.

> And I saw:
> when he opened the sixth seal,
> there was a violent earthquake.
> The sun turned black like haircloth
> and the whole of the moon became red like blood.
> The stars of heaven fell to earth
> as a fig tree buffeted by a great wind sheds its unripe figs.
> The sky was rolled up like a scroll
> and every mountain and island was displaced.
> The kings of the earth and the notables and the commanders,
> and the rich and the powerful,
> and all the slaves and the citizens hid themselves in caves
> and in the clefts of the mountains.
> They said to the hills and the rocks:
> Fall on us and hide us from the face of the one sitting on the throne
> and from the wrath of the lamb!
> For the great day of their wrath has come,

and who can stand it?
(Rev 6:12–17)

First of all, all the cosmic images of the de-creation of the world pass in review before us. As we have already noted, in the prophetic and apocalyptic literature these images do not refer primarily to material destruction but symbolize the disappearance of a "world," the end of a civilization. Then, rather than the destruction of human beings, as was described in the texts that speak of external anger, we see the distress of those who were involved in this world which is now on its way to oblivion. It is extremely significant that all the individuals mentioned are defined exclusively by their social role. They are unable to imagine what it could mean to exist in a different way, since their very identity has been bound up to such an extent with this world and its values.

This great upheaval is called "the great Day of the wrath of the one seated on the throne and of the lamb." Let us pause for a moment and consider the expression "the wrath of the lamb." Lambs are among the gentlest and most vulnerable animals that exist, and are not generally subject to fits of anger. Here we obviously have another of those paradoxical expressions that abound in this book. The slaughtered lamb, standing in the midst of God's throne, clearly represents Christ, dead and risen. At the heart of the Christian faith we find an unprecedented vision of the Messiah who, instead of conquering by the sword, does not avenge the violence of his enemies by violence in return, but instead shows love and forgiveness. This stupefying revelation of God and his representative on earth vanquishes those who believe in the law of "might makes right"; it sounds the death-knell of a society based on competition and the exploitation of the weakest.

In reality, the wrath of the lamb is his NO to the violence of evil, fully assumed and lived out to the very end. The day of wrath thus corresponds to Good Friday, considered in its deepest significance and confirmed by the good news of the resurrection. This does not mean, of course, that on one day, two thousand years ago, the old world vanished like the morning mist. That way of life unfortunately still continues, causing untold damage down through the centuries, sometimes even more intensely than before: "Woe to you, earth and sea, for the devil has come down to you in great fury, knowing that he has little time left" (12:12). But starting from the cross of Christ, the victory has already been achieved, a victory that continues throughout human history in the life of believers walking in the footsteps of their Master. "They have conquered by means of the blood of the lamb and the word of their testimony; they did not love their lives to the point of fearing death" (12:11). Love, manifested by the given life of Jesus the Messiah and expressed concretely by the shedding of his blood, is henceforth revealed as the driving force of history, a cause for rejoicing for those who accept it and a torment for those whose lives have been based on other foundations.

This paradoxical interpretation of God's wrath as the death of his Son consequently provides the key to understanding other parts of the book of Revelation. We have already noticed that, in this book, John alludes to a great many Old Testament passages. In particular, he evokes some that refer to the judgment of evildoers and the activity of divine anger. Taken in themselves, such passages seem to describe a violent act of destruction. But if we apply the true significance of the wrath of the Lamb to these texts, they take on a completely different aspect.

In chapter 14, for example, the seer describes the ultimate fate of human beings, described in terms of twofold harvest of the earth—of the grain and of the grapes. The symbol of the grain-harvest evokes, along the lines of its usage by Jesus (see Matt 9:37–38; 13:30; John 4:35–38), the righteous gathered into the kingdom of God. The act of crushing grapes in a winepress, however, has a less favorable meaning in the Hebrew Scriptures. It is used by the prophets to depict wrath coming upon God's enemies (Isa 63:1–6; Joel 4:13; Lam 1:15). Chapter 63 of the book of Isaiah is particularly violent in this regard: "I trod on them in my anger; I trampled them in my rage. Their juice spattered over my clothes and all my garments were polluted" (63:3). In the Apocalypse, we read:

> And the angel cast his sickle upon the earth,
> and he harvested the grapevine of the earth

and cast it into the great vat of the fury of God.
The vat was trampled outside the city,
and blood flowed from the vat
to the height of horses' bridles for a distance of 1,600 stadia.
(14:19–20)

As often in this book, it is apparently insignificant details that help us to understand the text. They are like a wink to the reader from someone hidden behind the scenery. Here, we read that "the vat was trampled outside the city" and this brings to mind Jesus who, "in order to sanctify the people by his own blood, suffered outside the gate" (Heb 13:12). The blood in question is therefore, once again, not the blood of the enemies, flowing as a result of an attack on God's part. It is rather Christ's blood, which recapitulates all the innocent blood shed throughout the centuries and lifts it up as a clear witness against the oppressors: "Every eye shall see him, including those who pierced him, and all the tribes of the earth will mourn over him" (Rev 1:7; cf. John 19:37; Zech 12:10). Does this refer to a final condemnation or is it a last call to conversion? The text remains indeterminate in this respect.

Similarly, in chapter 19 we witness the final battle against evil. Christ is described as a horseman mounted on a white horse, the archetype of humanity (cf. 6:2); he is followed by the armies of heaven. Here too there is an allusion to Isaiah 63: "He will trample the vat full of the wine of the furious wrath of God almighty" (19:15). Once again we find images of extreme violence, and once again two small details strike our attention. First of all, the sword with which the warrior strikes the nations is the sword of his mouth (cf. Isa 11:4)—in other words, he is victorious by his words of truth. And secondly, even before the combat begins, "he is clothed in a garment soaked in blood" (19:13).[1] Once again, the paradoxical victory of Christ on the cross leads to the eradication of evil and the disappearance of the wicked. Starting from Good

---

1. In Isaiah 63, the text also begins with the Judge who wears a garment stained with red. But then the text explains, in a flashback, that his clothing was stained by the grapes he trampled (63:3). Here, there is first of all the red mantle, and then comes the grape-harvest.

Friday and Easter Sunday, a new power has taken over the earth and is transforming everything from within.

It is time to conclude, and our conclusion is of the utmost importance. Despite the appearances, which are often contradictory, the book of Revelation confirms in its own way the vision of divine anger that we have found in the New Testament as a whole. External anger is present, but its essence is clearly unveiled as the self-destruction of evil. This process is necessary, but it is not sufficient, since its effects are purely negative. To reveal the fullness of his justice, God not only has to create a universe where evil ultimately destroys itself; God must in addition find an effective way to detach this evil from those who are in collusion with it, so that they are not eliminated along with it. This detaching is called forgiveness. In other words, to express it in a more traditional language, God must save people from their sins. But how can this forgiveness and this salvation become a reality within history? The Apocalypse replies: through "the one who loved us and freed us from our sins by his blood" (1:5; cf. 5:9). By his life given to the end, Christ cast evil "into the great vat of the wrath of God," which is nothing other than his cross. The human NO to God's NO is fully assumed from within, clothed in mercy and transformed into redemptive suffering. This, and this alone, is in the final analysis the wrath of a loving God.

Bibliography

Chenavier, Robert. *Simone Weil: L'attention au réel*. Paris: Michalon, 2009.
Grant, Deena E. *Divine Anger in the Hebrew Bible*. Catholic Biblical Quarterly Monograph Series 52. Washington, DC: Catholic Biblical Association of America, 2014.
Lewis, C. S. *The Great Divorce*. New York: HarperCollins, 2001.
Noffke, Suzanne. *The Letters of Catherine of Siena*. Vol. 2. Tempe: Arizona Center for Medieval and Renaissance Studies, 2001.
Sesboüé, Bernard. *Jésus-Christ l'Unique médiateur: Essai sur la rédemption et le salut*, Vol. 1. Paris: Desclée, 1988.
Weil, Simone. *Pensées sans ordre concernant l'amour de Dieu*. Paris: Gallimard, 1962.

Other Works Consulted

I did not find too much help in the biblical and theological literature on the topic of divine anger, at least concerning my particular slant on it, which is probably why one writes a book in the first place. The great exception is a work that captivated me when I encountered it many years ago, and to which I remain greatly indebted: Anthony Tyrell Hanson, *The Wrath of the Lamb* (London: SPCK, 1957); after sixty years it can still be read with enormous profit. Another more recent overview, also very helpful, is offered by Ralf Miggelbrink, *Der zornige Gott: Die Bedeutung einer anstößigen biblischen Tradition* (Darmstadt: Wissenschaftliche Buchgesellschaft, 2002). See also his *Der Zorn Gottes: Geschichte und Aktualität einer ungeliebten biblischen Tradition* (Freiburg: Herder, 2000).

Two monographs provided important information for my work: Deena E. Grant, *Divine Anger in the Hebrew Bible* (see above); and Samantha Joo, *Provocation and Punishment: The Anger of God in the Book of Jeremiah and Deuteronomistic Theology*, Beihefte zur Zeitschrift für die alttestamentliche Wissenschaft (Berlin: Walter de Gruyter, 2006).

Regarding Marcion I used especially Sebastian Moll, *The Arch-Heretic Marcion*, Wissenschaftliche Untersuchungen zum NT, 250 (Tübingen: Mohr Siebeck, 2010). And for the story of the ark, the fascinating reflections of Walter Brueggemann, *Ichabod Toward Home: The Journey of God's Glory* (Grand Rapids MI: Eerdmans, 2002; reprint, Eugene, OR: Wipf & Stock, 2005), offer much food for thought. Finally, concerning the transformation of anger into suffering by the prophets, see the luminous lines of Joseph Ratzinger (Pope Benedict XVI), *Daughter Zion* (San Francisco, CA: Ignatius, 1983), 22–23.

Scripture Index

OLD TESTAMENT

Genesis

1:31	66
30:2	23

Exodus

3:2	18
7–11	110
15:8–10	19
19:10–11, 22	20
19:12–13	20
19:16, 18	20
19:21–24	20
25:10–16	12
34:5–7	63
34:6	3, 33, 54

Numbers

10:33–36	12
14:18	63

Deuteronomy

8:6	8
10:1–5	12
10:12	8

Joshua

15:8	79

Judges

2:11–21	53
2:14	75
3:9	53
3:15	53
14:19	24

1 Samuel

4:1–11	13
4:4	12
5:1–5	13
5:6–12	13
6:19a	13
6:19–20	13
20:30–34	24

2 Samuel

6:2	14
6:6–7	14
6:8	14
6:11–12	14

1 Kings

3:16–28	69
8:46	75
19:11–12	16

2 Kings

13:5	53
17:15	55
21:2–15	55
22 – 23	52
22:15–17	55
23:26–27	1, 55

2 Chronicles

6:36	75
36:16–17	75

Nehemiah

9:17	63
11:30	79

Job

1:1	58
4:7–9	58
9:20	58
12:9	58
15:20–35	58
18:5-21	58
19:11	58
19:25–27	59
20:4–29	58
21	58
22	58
27:5–6	58
42:7	59

Psalms

10:9	56
10:12	56
10:17	56
13:2–3	56
16:5	109
22:26	56
23:5	109
28:2	56
29:4–5	17
29:7	17
29:8–9	17
29:11	18
34:6	56
35:1	56
35:10	56
37:2	57
37:3	57
37:7	57
37:34	57
43:1	61
49:15	57
49:17,19	57
62:12	77
68:7–9	17
68:24–25	17
73:13	56–57
73:25–26	57
75:8	101, 109
78:58–61	75
83:1–2	56
83:13–15	18
86:15	63
95:10–11	97
103:8	63
106:40–41	75
116:13	109
140:12	56
143:2	77
145:8	63

Proverbs

14:17	30
14:29	30
15:1	30
15:18	30
16:32	30
22:24	30
29:22	30
30:16	86

Qoheleth (Ecclesiastes)

2:24	58
3:17	58

3:20	58	2:2	47
3:22	58	2:5	55
5:17	58	2:20	47
7:15	58	2:30	45
7:16–17	58	2:35	45
8:10–14	58	3:1–5	47
8:15	58	3:20	47
9:2	58	3:12	45
9:7–10	58	4:4	45
11:9	58	4:7	45
12:13	58	4:8,26	45
		4:19	47

Song of Songs

8:6–7	86	5:3	45
		5:25	45
		6:11	47
		7:20	45

Isaiah

1:10–18	40	8:7	45
2:6–22	40	8:18,21,23	47
2:12	40	9:25	45
2:19, 21	40	10:10	45
5:25	2, 40	10:19	48
6	40	12:13	45
6:5	41	13:17	47, 101
9:11, 16, 20	40	14:17	47, 101
10:4	40	15:10	47–48
10:5	41	15:17	47
10:24–25	41	15:18	48
11:4	118	16:1–9	47
12:1	41	16:2	47
13:9–13	42	17:4	45
14:1	41	19	93
26:20–21	42	20:7–8	48
29:6	42	20:9	48
30:27–33	41	21:5,12	45
34:2	41	23:9	48
55:8–9	20, 43	23:20	45
57:15	43	25:30	45
63:1–6	117	29:11	45
63:3	117, 118n1	30:14	47
		30:24	45
		31:20	50, 96
		32:37–41	46

Jeremiah

1:6	45	44:7–8	54–55
1:10	45	49:37	45

Jeremiah (*continued*)

50:13	45
51:45	45

Lamentations

1:15	117
3:33	69

Ezekiel

5	93
18	64
20:33	25
21:36	75
34:17,20	69

Daniel

7:9-11	61

Hosea

1:2	44
2	93
2:5-15	48
2:16, 21-22	48
2:17	44
5:14	44
8:5	44
11:1-6	49
11:8	96
11:8-9	49
11:10	44
13:7-8	44

Joel

2:13	63
4:13	117

Amos

1	38
1:2	38, 39
2:2,5	38
2:10	39
2:15	38
3:7	39
3:7-8	39
3:8, 12	39
3:13	39
3:14	38
4:12	38
4:13 3x	39
5:5,27	38
5:6	38
5:8	39
5:14-16 2x	39
5:17	38
5:18,20	39
5:19	39
5:21	39
5:27	39
6:7	38
6:8 2x	38, 39
6:14	39
7:4	38
7:14-15	37
7:17	38
8:4-8	38
8:8	38
9:5	38
9:6	39
9:10	38

Jonah

1:9	60
4:1-2	60
4:2	63
4:6-8	60
4:9-10	62

Zephaniah

1:15	76

Zechariah

12:10	118

Malachi

4:1–2	46, 88

Sirach (Ecclesiasticus)

35:12–14	61

∼

NEW TESTAMENT

Matthew

3:12	79
4:10	91
5:5	103
5:22	91
7:1–7	93
7:2	87
7:23	92
7:24–27	82
8:12	79
9:37–38	117
10:15	78
11:16–17	97
11:20–24	98
11:22–24	78
12:34	92
12:36	78
12:38–39	93
12:39	97
12:41–42	78
13:30	117
13:40	79
13:48	80
14:31	97
15:1–9	91
16:4	97
16:5–12	97
16:23	92
22:13	79
23:1–36	91
23:35	115
23:37–39	99
24	77
24:3	77
24:22	112
24:51	79
25:30	79
25:31–46	61, 78
26:37	100
26:38	101
26:39	4

Mark

1:25	91
1:40–43	95
2:22	72
3:5	96
4:39	91
6:5–6	97
8:12	97
8:14–21	97
8:33	92
9:18–19	97
9:42	92
9:43–47	92
9:44–48	79
10:14	92
11:12–21	94
12:1–12	94
13	77
13:26	78
14:33	100
14:34	101

Luke

2:40	4
4:35	91
4:41	91
6:20–26	98
7:31–32	97
9:52–55	92
10:12–15	78
10:13–15	98
11:23	76

Luke (continued)

11:29–32	93
11:31–32	78
11:37–54	91
12:5	79
13:1–5	73
13:9	80
13:28	79
13:34–35	99
14:15–24	80
17	77
17:22–37	77
19:21	87
19:22	87
19:41–42	99
21	77
22:44	100
24:21	71
24:27	72

John

1:11	6
1:14	43
3:10	97
3:16–17	83
3:18	84
3:19–21	84
3:36	76, 87
4:35–38	117
4:48	93
5:22, 24	78–79
5:24	88
5:29	78
5:40	84
6:37	84
9:1–3	73
9:39–41	85
10:5	92
10:30	105
11:33	102
11:35	102
12:27	100
12:46–48	84

12:48	78
13:21	100
13:26–27, 30	85
14:9	97
15:6	80
18:11	101
19:34	113
19:37	118

Romans

1:17	75
1:18	75
1:18–32	74
1:24, 26, 28	75
2:3–4	75–76
2:5	76
2:6	77
2:6–11	81
4:15	74
5:9	73
6:16	74
7:10	74
8:1	88, 106
15:19	71

1 Corinthians

1:8	81
3:10–15	82
4:5	76, 81
13:12	5
15:28	86

2 Corinthians

1:19	85
1:20	8
2:15	74
3:6	5
3:12–18	5
3:16	5, 109
4:3	74
5:10	81
10:5	72

Galatians

1:4	74
2:4	3
4:4	6

Ephesians

1:9–10	108
4:26–27	31
5:6	76

Philippians

| 1:6 | 81 |

Colossians

2:9	5
3:6	76
3:25	81

1 Thessalonians

1:10	73, 103
3:2	71
5:3	81
5:9	73

2 Thessalonians

1:8–9	81
2	81
2:10	74

2 Timothy

| 1:10 | 105 |

Hebrews

9:27	81
10:16–31	81
10:25	81
12:26–29	82–83
13:12	118

James

1:8	83
1:19–20	30
2:13	81, 87
4:8	83
5:3	76
5:12	81

1 Peter

| 1:17 | 81 |
| 4:5 | 81 |

2 Peter

2:20–22	81
3:10–12	102
3:13	76, 103

1 John

1:5	85
3:14	88
4:8, 16	84
4:17	78
4:18	105–6

Revelation

1:5	108, 119
1:7	118
2:26	114
3:14	108
4–6	111
5:5	113
5:6	113
5:8	115
5:9	119
5:9–10	113
6:1–8	111
6:2	118
6:8	112
6:9	115
6:11	115
6:12–17	115–16
7:9	114

Revelation (*continued*)

7:14	114
8:3–5	115
8:7–12	112
9:1–12	111
9:13–21	111
9:20–21	112
10:3–4	112
11:18	110
12:11	114, 117
12:12	117
13:10	114
14:4	114
14:10	109
14:12	114
14:19–20	117–18
14:20	113
16	112
16:1	110
16:11	112
16:19	109
17:4	110
18:3	110
18:6	110
18:24	115
19:13	118
19:15	118
21:3	109

CPSIA information can be obtained
at www.ICGtesting.com
Printed in the USA
LVHW111103101022
730344LV00012B/194